Harvesting Nature's Bounty©

A guidebook of nature lore, wild edible, medicinal, and utilitarian plants and animals.

Harvesting Nature's Bounty©

A guidebook of nature lore, wild edible, medicinal, and utilitarian plants and animals.

By

Kevin F. Duffy

Copyright © 1998, 2000 by Kevin F. Duffy

All rights reserved.
No part of this book may be reproduced, stored in a retrieval system, or transmitted by any means, electronic, mechanical, photocopying, recording, or otherwise, without written permission from the author.

ISBN: 1-58721-876-3

About The Book

Harvesting Nature's Bounty is a treasure trove of nature wisdom and lore. It not only covers wild edible and medicinal plants, and survival skills, it also covers subjects as varied as fish stunners, weather predictors, cricket temperature, pine pitch glue, natural bug repellents, and a wide variety of exciting new culinary sources.

This book will show you how to commune with nature and reconnect at a level known only our distant ancestors. This book will empower the reader with the knowledge and resources needed to begin their re-connection back to the Earthmother. The reader will learn where the treasures of nature are located and how they can be used. The reader will also learn how to assist nature in her recovery as they learn. As the reader begins to see nature at deeper level they will begin to recognize all of her inhabitants both large and small and see the significant role each play in the big scheme. When this happens, the reader will never look at a field, forest, or blade of grass the same ever again.

Over **200 species** are discussed along with their various uses. Several articles have been published in various magazines and newsletters based on this research. This book is <u>heavily annotated with references</u>. In addition to the research, most of the accounts are from first hand experience and approximately **100 supporting photographs** are included. This book offers a <u>unique collection of Nature Lore</u> available nowhere else.

There are other books covering various aspects referenced in *Harvesting Nature's Bounty*, such as wild edible plant identification books. There is no other single book that covers the breadth of nature lore including edible, medicinal, utilitarian plant uses. Also included in this book is a wide range of other unique nature lore including little known useful tricks used primarily by Native Americans. Several aspects of wilderness survival including shelters, fire starting, water collecting, alternative hunting methods without weapons are also covered. This book is a cornucopia of nature lore that will have a wide appeal to anyone interested in any aspect of nature. If you ever wanted to know the answers to any of the following questions then this book is for you:

Do you want to know how to eat a pine tree?

Do you think you don't have any wild edible or medicinal plants near you? Think again! The author of this book found over thirty in his very unexceptional small suburban lot.

Do you know where and how to safely collect wild edible and medicinal plants without hurting nature's delicate balance? This book will not only show you how, but will tell you how to enhance nature's garden.

Would you like to learn how to find and eat some the most important food staples of the Native Americans, like acorns, groundnuts, cattails, and others?

Wouldn't you like to know how to build a survival shelter with no tools that can protect you and keep you dry in sub-freezing weather?

Do you want to know how to catch large bullfrogs during the day without any tools or weapons?

Would you like to know about a plant that will prevent poison ivy from developing after you have been exposed?

Would you like to know how to find wild edible plants in the dead of winter?

Did you know that North America's largest native fruit can't be purchased in any grocery store? It can only be found in nature.

Have you ever tried North America's largest berry. It too can't be found any grocery store. It is also as sweet as any candy you have ever eaten.

Would you like to know about natural treatments that can be found in nature for over dozens of the most common complaints? According to the latest scientific studies cited in this book, some of these remedies may be more effective and safer than anything man-made.

Did you know that many of the European settlers died from scurvy while living in the midst of many plant species that have a greater abundance of easily obtainable vitamin C than orange juice?

Do you have a headache and want some quick relief from nature?

Would you like to know how to make epoxy glue from natural sources?

Did you know there is a plant growing in your lawn that is more nutritious than any vegetable you can find in the grocery store and this plant is available in nature year-round?

Would you like to know how to stun fish with natural plant substances and have them float to the surface for easy collection.

Would you like to know about natural plant sources that can be used for bug repellents? They also smell good as well and a lot of them can also be eaten.

Would you like to impress your friends, show them how you can tell the temperature by listening to the crickets?

Would you like to know about an aquatic plant that prevents the growth of mosquito larvae in its presence?

Would you like to know how to get safe water from nature?

Would you like to know how to collected large edible crayfish with just a flashlight and a bucket at night?

Would you like to find natural wild substitutes for the majority of the spices in your spice rack?

Would you like to be introduced to an abundant wild relative of spinach that taste a whole lot better and is significantly more nutritious?

Did you know that many flowers growing in your yard might be edible?

Table of Contents

Preface xiii
Disclaimer xv
Introduction xvii

Chapter 1: Foraging - The Free Lunch 1
   Where To Forage 1
   The Broccoli Theory 3
   Foraging Ethics 3
   Edible Wild Plants Foraging Guidelines 5

Chapter 2: The Big Ten 7
   The Big First: The Oaks 7
   Shelling 8
   Leaching Tannic Acid From Acorns 8
   Other Oak Foods 8
   What To Do With Leached Acorns 8
   The Big Second: The Pines 9
   Pine Pollen 10
   Pine Nuts 10
   Other Evergreens 11
   The Big Third: The Grasses 11
   Author Standing In Front Of Phragmites 13
   Wild Rice 14
   The Big Fourth: Cattails 15
   The Big Fifth: Dandelion 20
   The Big Sixth: Prickly Pear Cactus 21
   The Big Seventh: Lamb's-Quarters 22
   The Big Eighth: Nettles 24
   The Big Ninth: Mustards 25
   The Big Tenth: Berries: Brambles And Blueberries 26
   Brambles 26
   Blueberries 27

Chapter 3: Aquatic Wild Edibles 29
   Mints 29
   Chufa 29
   Groundnut 29
   Sweetflag 31
   American Lotus 31
   Arrowhead 32
   Reed 33
   Great Bulrush 33
   Wild Rice 33
   Duckweed 34

    Water Purity 34

Chapter 4: Wet Forest Edibles 37
    Year-Round 37
    Spring And Early Summer 40
    Devil's Walking Stick 50
    Summer 53
    Fall-Winter 53
    Pawpaw 54
    Persimmons 57
    Mayapple 61
    Nodding Wild Onion 62

Chapter 5: Disturbed Areas 65
    Poke 65
    Elderberry 67
    Purslane 68
    Day-Lilies 69
    Chickweed 71
    Yucca 71
    Burdock 72
    Amaranth 72

Chapter 6: Culinary Substitutes 73
    Salt And Pepper 73
    Sugar 74
    Coffee 76
    Teas 77
    Garlic 79
    Onion 80
    Lemon 80
    Carrot 80
    Thickeners 84
    Gelatin And Pectin 84
    Ginger And Cinnamon 84
    Horseradish 85
    Poppy And Sesame Seed 85
    Parsnips 85
    Rennet 86
    Allspice 86

Chapter 7: Winter Foods 89
    Latent Fall Crops 89
    Persistent Winter Edibles 89
    Late Winter Arrivals 90
    Underground Edibles 91
    Jerusalem Artichoke 91

    Garlic Mustard 92
    Go To The Water 92

Chapter 8: Critters 93
    Water Critters 93
    Frogs 93
    Snapping Turtles 95
    Catfish 97
    Crayfish 97
    Clams 98
    Land Critters 99
    Crayfish 99
    Possums 99
    Insects 100

Chapter 9: Wilderness Medicine 101
    Daily Annoyances 101
    Headaches/Aches/Pains/Fever 101
    Cuts/Burns/Abrasions 102
    Heartburn 104
    Hay Fever 105
    Decongestant 106
    Assaults From The Plant Kingdom 107
    Poison Ivy/Oak/Sumac 107
    Nettles 107
    Assaults From The Animal Kingdom 108
    Insect Bites And Stings 108
    Tick Bites 109
    A Word About Lyme Disease 109
    Spider Bites 109
    Snake Bites 109
    The Little Beasties 110
    Fungus 110
    Lice 110
    Worms 110
    Cold Sores 111
    Warts 112
    Coughs 113
    Bacterial Infections 114
    Nausea/Motion Sickness 114
    Diarrhea 115
    Constipation 115
    Hemorrhoids 116
    Eye Problems 116
    Ear Aches 117
    Flu And Colds 117
    Depression 117

    Stimulants 117
    Sedatives 118
    Keeping Healthy 118
    Nutrition Enhancers 118
    High Blood Pressure 119
    High Cholesterol 119
    Immune Enhancers/Adaptogens 120

Chapter 10: Natural Pest Controls 121
    Diet 121
    Biological Warfare 121
    Gardens 122
    Other Pest Controls 123

Chapter 11: Nature's Bag Of Tricks 125
    The Bow Drill 125
    Basketry 128
    Pine Pitch Glue 128
    Shelters 130
    Wickiup: A Shelter For All Seasons 130
    Debris Hut 131
    Scout Pit 133
    Fish Stunners 134
    Soaps And Deodorants 135
    Soaps 135
    Deodorants And Perfumes 135
    Water, Water Everywhere 135
    Toiletries 137
    Weather Predictors 138
    Cricket Temperature 139
    Odds And Ends 139
    Cordage 139
    Pan Scrubbers, Fingernail Files, And Sandpaper 141
    Torches 141
    Pollution Indicators 141

Chapter 12: Wild Farming 143
    Bibliography 147
    Appendix A: Favorite References 153
    Appendix B: Where To Buy 157
    Appendix C: Schools 163
    Appendix D: Videos 169
    General Index 171

We need the tonic of wildness - to wade sometimes in marshes where the bittern and the meadow-hen lurk, and hear the booming of the snipe; to smell the whispering sedge where only some wilder and more solitary fowl builds her nest, and the mink crawls with its belly close to the ground. At the same time that we are earnest to explore and learn all things, we require that all things be mysterious and unexplorable, that land and sea be infinitely wild, unsurveyed and unfathomed by us because unfathomable. We can never have enough of nature.

Henry David Thoreau

Preface

With so many plant identification and foraging books available, why another book on this diverse subject? Most plant use books are organized by plant species and overwhelm the reader with hundreds of species at once. They also generally are narrowly focused on one aspect of plant use such as edible or medicinal. This book also presents hundreds of plants, but is organized in a manner to allow the reader to focus his attention a little bit at a time on specific areas of interest. This book is also not narrowly focused on just one functional area. It covers a myriad of other uses of plants, animals, and other aspects of nature. After reading chapter one, which covers the basics, chapter two covers the Big Ten. This top-ten plant group is a great introduction to wild edible plants, as they are generally easy to recognize and find in abundance. They also form a great baseline to build your ethnobotanical knowledge base. This is the book I wished I had owned some 30 years ago when I first started my long quest into nature. It is also the reference I desire today as I continue my wilderness education.

This book is not a plant identification book. There are lots of pictures in this book along with plant identification details. The purpose of these is to quickly narrow your search to a candidate species to be verified in other plant identification books. The added details in this book are there to enhance or reinforce details found in identification books. There are many wonderful plant identification books readily available in bookstores and libraries. I strongly urge anyone interested in foraging to familiarize themselves with one or more of the outstanding references listed in the appendices and bibliography. At a very minimum, the Peterson's Wild Edible Plant book is a must in any forager's library. This book and others should be used if a more in depth knowledge of a particular species is desired.

When conducting the research for this book, I soon realized I had gained much of my knowledge from personal experience. I also found many others had little jewels of information sprinkled throughout the literature. However, I could find no single source that provided the broad spectrum of highly interesting tidbits I was looking for. This book is an attempt to capture the lion's share of what I considered to be the most interesting and useful jewels of nature lore into one volume. Wherever applicable, the source of unique information is referenced to the bibliography. In many instances the information is widely available and cannot be attributed to one author. Every attempt was made to make information contained in this book as accurate and up to date as possible.

My quest for knowledge about nature does not end with the completion of this book; it only just begins. My deepest hopes are that this book becomes your springboard as well, as you continue your nature education.

Disclaimer

Collecting and eating wild foods carries with it certain inherent risks including but not limited to misidentification, allergic reactions, pesticides, pollutants, or over indulgence. If you are not absolutely sure of a plant's identification take it to a qualified expert such as a county extension officer or botanist for verification. Once a new plant has been positively identified, eat sparingly to ensure you do not have an allergic reaction. Whenever any new food is introduced to your body for the first time, either wild or domestic, there is a danger of an allergic reaction. Allergic reactions can be fatal. Some plants have poison look alikes such as the edible Wild Carrot and its' poison look alike Poison Hemlock. Other plants have poison parts as well, such as Mayapple. Many of our domestic plants, such as the common "Irish" potato, which is a member of the Nightshade family, are also poisonous. Apple and cherry seeds contain cyanide. Still other plants have poison in them during certain parts of their life cycle like poke and asparagus that both become poisonous upon maturation. Others have suspected carcinogens such as sassafras and common mushrooms (Agaricus bisporus) purchased in the grocery store.

I am neither a medical doctor nor nutritionist. The edibility and medicinal properties presented in this book are for informational and educational purposes only. Neither the publisher nor myself assume any liability for the use or misuse of information contained herein.

Introduction

In God's wildness lies the hope of the world — the great fresh unblighted, unredeemed wilderness.

John Muir

Today we live in a highly dependent society that has traded expedience for simplicity, self-sufficiency and purity. Most Americans jump into their fossil fueled vehicles and drive to the local grocery store to buy raw and prepared foods. These foods have been grown using fossil fuel based pesticides and fertilizers. Additionally, other unnatural preservatives, antibiotics and now genetically engineered organisms have been introduced. The components and end products at the grocery and pharmaceutical industries are more often than not shipped thousand of miles in fossil-fueled conveyances before reaching their point-of-sale. This all adds up to gross inefficiencies in wasted fuels and devastating environmental damage. Admittedly everyone cannot become a forager, but just as many individuals do their small part by recycling, responsible foraging can also play a vital role in contributing a small part to improving our little planet.

Native peoples had no dependence on any society for daily sustenance. They lived as an integral part of nature in which they viewed themselves as an inseparable part of a whole. They felt water, which flowed through their streams, was no different than the blood that flowed through their veins. They would no more dump waste into the rivers than they would put it into their bodies, because in the end they understood that these two actions had the same result. A Native American of old, could travel across this continent with nothing more than his hand-crafted loincloth, knife and bow and want for nothing. He would not want for shelter, water, fire, clothing or loneliness. He was a natural part of his surroundings.

Modern man has lost his familiarity and intimacy with nature. In Robert Heinlein's classic novel "Stranger in a Strange Land," intelligent sailboat-like Martians raise the main character on Mars from a baby until adulthood. He returns to Earth as an adult with all of his mental references from the Martian society. He is truly an alien to earth. Modern man is also a stranger in a strange land when it comes to his natural place on Earth. Most of the body of natural knowledge is alien to modern man. Fortunately there has been a recent popularization and rekindling of nature awareness. The earlier pioneers of this movement included such notorieties as Euell Gibbons and Bradford Angier. More recently many others have joined in the fight to preserve this knowledge. It is not too late to reclaim our forgotten legacy and rekindle our relationship with the Earth Mother.

Occasionally there will be cautions associated with each plant such as poison look-alikes, poison plant parts, suspected or actual poisons and carcinogens. Wherever possible I have included these cautions. The cautions are not all inclusive and they never could be, as new discoveries about food safety are continually discovered. Please read these cautions very carefully and if you desire further information about a particular plant consult the bibliography. Some of the most nutritious vegetables available are wild ones such as Dandelion, Amaranth, and Lamb's-quarters. These three are all in the top four of the most nutritious vegetables known as measured by the USDA. These can rarely be found in grocery stores. Throughout this book, there will be cautions or warnings to known or suspected hazards that have been found from other sources.

Many of the cautions in this book may allude to suspected or known carcinogens. I find these cautions particularly interesting because we are inundated with natural and manmade carcinogens throughout our lives. Unfortunately most carcinogen risk factors are extrapolated from massive doses in animals over a short duration of time to small doses in humans over a long duration. This extrapolation makes at least two large leaps of faith. The first is that a carcinogen in an animal will necessarily also be a carcinogen in humans. The second is the presumption that if an excessive exposure to a substance over a short period of time results in cancer, that it follows a small exposure to the same substance over a long period will likewise cause cancer. When suspected carcinogens are from a natural source that is already established in our culture, like cigarettes, alcohol, or mushrooms there is no hue and cry about banning them. On the other hand, if a carcinogen is from a manmade or insignificant natural source, it is banned from sale despite the relatively small risk of cancer. I do not advocate ignoring any cautions regarding food safety and all should be taken seriously. However, I also do not advocate trying to totally avoid everything that has an associated risk. I still occasionally eat store bought mushrooms, but in moderation. I will continue to enjoy other foods, both domestic and wild, with a relatively low carcinogen risk in moderation. Anything taken in excess could potentially result in a danger to our bodies.

Throughout this book common names will be used wherever possible with the scientific names following in parenthesis. The scientific name is the only unambiguous method of positively referencing an individual plant species. Even though these scientific names are harder to pronounce and remember, they provide essential information through their uniqueness and their ready association with other species that are close relatives. Whenever a scientific name is listed with *spp.* at the end, this is referring to the genus or collection species belonging to a particular genus. For example Typha spp. refers to plant species belonging to the Cattail genus Typha, e.g., Typha angustifolia, Typha latifolia, and Typha glauca. In some instances the scientific name is the common name such as Ginkgo biloba, which is commonly known as Ginkgo or Ginkgo tree. Common names also serve a vital role, particularly when trying to speak to someone not familiar with scientific names of particular species. However, the pitfall is that each species often has many common names and many common names are given to entirely different species. Pigweed, for example, refers to both Amaranthus species (Amaranth) and Chenopodium album (Lamb's-quarters). The most common name or the common name with which the author is most familiar will be listed as well as the scientific name.

The Creator has given us everything we need to live on this earth. It us up to every one of us to ensure we do not destroy this great gift. We are all part of a whole that is greater than the sum of its parts.

Chapter 1: Foraging - The Free Lunch

Manna from Heaven

And when the children of Israel saw it, they said one to another, It is manna: for they wist not what it was. And Moses said unto them, This is the bread, which the LORD hath given you to eat.

Exodus 16:15

What is foraging? Foraging is the gathering of foodstuffs found in nature's pantry or harvesting of wild plants and animals, exclusive of hunting and fishing. There are some examples of gathering fish and other animals with minimal tools, which will be included in this general definition of foraging. The term grazing refers to the act of eating as you forage. This is almost an unavoidable consequence of foraging and, sometimes, a full belly of natures finest, will be the only fruits of your effort.

It is estimated that there are approximately 20,000 plants in Canada and the United States (Elias, 1982), another 30,000 in Mexico and another 300,000 in South and Central America. Only 150 species are cultivated on a commercial scale and a mere twenty feed the vast majority of our planet. There are approximately 20,000 species that have edible parts worldwide (Facciola, 1990). The Native Americans used at least 1112 food plants (Duke, 1992). With all this food free for the picking, why would anyone want to settle for the common twenty or even the elusive 150 cultivated species. To be certain there are many cultivars of these 150 species. For example there are 8000 cultivars of apple, although most people are only familiar with a dozen or so (Facciola, 1990).

Throughout the book, comparisons of flavor may be made between wild food and more familiar domesticated varieties. This is very similar to the often-heard comparison that a particular game tastes like chicken or beef. However, anyone who has ever eaten venison knows that it tastes like venison and only similar to beef and squirrel tastes like squirrel and only similar to chicken. These comparisons will be made from time to time to give the reader an appreciation for what the author and others believe a particular food tastes like. Your personal experience may or may not agree with these findings. This discovery of the different is one of the pleasures of foraging.

Where to Forage

The first step in foraging is to find a place to forage. Wherever you forage make sure the environment in which you find them is safe. Some examples of unsafe environments are power line easements, within 50 feet of heavily traveled roads and anywhere chemicals may be applied to the flora, either by accident or design. Power line easements are inherently unsafe due to the application of herbicides to curb tree growth. The same applies to railroad easements and any other easement where tree growth is controlled without a mower or animals. These applications of chemicals may not be obvious as many are applied at night by aircraft. Heavily traveled roads are also dangerous as the plant life near them acts as filters for all the exhaust and applied road chemicals. You have probably heard that planting trees help clean the air. All plant life helps to clean the air. Just as your lungs absorb impurities from the air so do plants. It is estimated the heavy metal content may be up to twenty times greater in plants located near heavily traveled roads (Gail, 1990). As the distance between the plants and the road increases, the heavy metal content decreases. Harvest at least fifty to seventy five feet away from these roads where heavy metal content diminishes to normal levels.

There are also dangers from the very place where much of our produce originates, the farm. The farmstead may present dangers due to high concentrations of nitrates that some plants, like Lamb's-quarters (Chenopodium album), Purslane (Portulaca oleracea), Chickweed (Stellaria media), and others absorb to toxic levels. Dangers similar to those discussed in the lawn and easement examples may also be present. Just be careful and thoughtful where you forage.

Always ask permission before foraging on private property. You will probably get some funny looks or comments when you ask if you can pull up some of their weeds so you can eat them. It is equally important to ensure foraging is an allowable activity when using public property.

In any event, you probably will not have to look far to find a good foraging area. Start in your own backyard, assuming you have not poisoned it with pesticides and weed killers. When I look at a weedy yard, I see a free produce market, where most people see a weedy yard.

The herbicide industry has convinced most consumers that a manicured lawn of lush weed free grass is a desirable healthy plot of earth. Nothing could be further from the truth. The next time you go into a lawn and garden center, take a close look at the warnings on those pesticide products. There are many times more words devoted to the hazards of these products than to their application. The other prevalent type of products promoted by the industry are various dicot killers which prey upon the evil dicots (non-grasses), e.g., dandelion and its cohort in crime, plantain. It makes me cringe to see these two wonderful plants maligned. Destroying all plant life except for the monocot grasses results in a monoculture that is unnatural and unsustainable. A manicured lawn is basically a wasteland in nature's balance.

If your yard meets the sanity test for purity and is wonderfully under maintained and filled with nasty weeds such as dandelion and plantain, you have found your first foraging area. You may be thinking that this will not be much of a foraging opportunity. Think again. Along with a house in which we used to live in northern Virginia, was a small quarter acre lot. I often had people compliment me on the nice lawn I had. I am telling you this, because I do not want you to think that I lived with a lawn that looked like an abandoned lot. This neighborhood was strictly Middle America. The only applications I made to my yard were spring fertilizer without weed killers and occasional water after weeks with no rain. I found the following useful plants growing in this average yard within a one year period:

Dandelions	Peppermint	Wintercress	Mulberry	Sweetgum
Poke	Chickweed	Violets	Prickly Lettuce	Yellow Dock
Maple	Catnip	Bull Thistle	Plantains (2)	Red Clover
Garlic	Henbit	Ground Ivy	Russian Olive	Indian Strawberry
Burdock	Puffballs	Blackberry	Crab Apples	Wood Sorrel
Mustard	Mullein	Field Onion	Lamb's-quarters	Purslane
White Pine	Indian Mallow	Wild Carrot		

I will not even try to describe the amount of wild edibles I have found on large parcel of land I own in southern Indiana. In fact I will spend the rest of my life trying to discover them all and go to my grave knowing I missed many.

Wait! Before you run out the back door and start grazing on everything in sight, you must first take care of **the most important facet of foraging**, positive identification. Please read the disclaimer! This book is not an identification book. A good identification book is a must, regardless of whether you have an expert to help or not. Read the entire introduction section first. I know this may go against your basic instincts, (particularly if you are a man) but this is one case where reading the instructions is a necessity. There are lots of valuable nuggets in the introductory sections. When you read the description of a plant, read and confirm it all. Make sure every detail is the same. Do not rely solely on the pictures. If there is a poison look alike listed, find a description and picture of it as well. Cross-reference the plant in two or more books.

It is no accident that the easier to use identification books are primarily keyed upon the flowers. Hint, Hint. Using the flowers as the primary discriminator is usually the easiest way to identify a plant. There are many outstanding identification books available, several of which are listed in Appendix-A and the bibliography. I take at least two of these most of the time when I go foraging. I also frequently refer to the other references listed in the bibliography. Some of the other references can be less user-friendly like Gray's Manual of Botany, but do not get discouraged. These books also add another dimension of identification and often lead to the more subtle differences within a genus.

Universities, wildlife refuges, forests, parks, sanctuaries, and agricultural stations may have individuals available to give talks or wild food walks. Take advantage of any local expertise or enroll in a class. For a more complete list of resources see Appendix A.

The Broccoli Theory

I have developed a theory, which I call the Broccoli Theory that I use with people who give me a blank stare when I point out a wild edible plant. The blank stare tells me that they think recognizing a wild plant in its native environs is nothing short of impossible. I ask them if they think they could recognize broccoli, if it were growing in the same spot. The answer to date has been yes. In the not-too-distant future, as mankind distances itself further and further from nature, the answer may become no. The reason most people could differentiate broccoli from the surrounding flora is because it is familiar.

Wild edible plants are not familiar to most, but once you get to know them they are. Start with something somewhat familiar, like dandelion. This plant is familiar not as a food and medicine to most, but as common weed. As always make sure you positively identified, with one of the plant identification books. Validate every characteristic, feel it, smell it. Look at variation from plant to plant. Once you have positively identified it, try adding it to your evening meal. Prepare it different ways off and on for a week. At the end of that week, dandelion will be yours. You now own Dandelion. Pick one or two different plant species a week and add them to your collection of plants you own. Just take it one plant at a time and soon you own hundreds of new plants.

Foraging Ethics

Foraging ethics is a topic that must not be overlooked. When the European settlers came to this country, they viewed the wilderness as something that needed to be tamed or conquered, i.e, roads, manicured lawns, forests chopped down, animals hunted, etc. The European philosophy of the wilderness resulted in the decimation of the carrier pigeon, the near dissemination of the American Bison, and extinction of untold hundreds of other species.

Native Americans on the other hand, viewed nature as a gift from the Creator that was inseparable from them. The water in the streams was the same as the blood in their veins and they showed it no less respect. Their philosophy of man's role with nature was that of the caretaker and nurturer. Man could harvest from nature, but in return he must assist in the process of keeping nature in balance. The Native American always thought in terms of seven generations in the future. He would ask himself if what he were doing today, was in the best interests of his offspring seven generations from now. He would pray to a plant before collecting, in essence, ask its permission. He would offer it a gift such as prayer or maybe some tobacco and thank the plant and the Creator for their generosity. If it were in seed he would plant some of its seeds. He would only collect from abundant sources, never depleting, but rather thinning the population to ensure its continued health, a truly novel concept for the western mind.

Whenever I teach someone about foraging, I also teach him or her to respect these gifts from the Creator and to adopt the Native American philosophy of nature. Never over harvest a plant or animal. Never wastes anything collected from nature, if you aren't going to use it leave it alone. Be careful of trampling on delicate plants, they have feelings too. The Earth Mother will provide everything you need for sustenance and health. It us up to us to demonstrate our gratitude for this great gift.

KISS

KISS is among the many acronyms used in the Navy. It expands to Keep It Simple Stupid. This acronym was developed as a result of the tendency of military projects to become more complex than necessary. As complexity increased so did delays, costs, and problems. In order to combat complexity, the military came up with KISS, which means decide what you really want and leave off the bells and whistles. Bells and whistles only drive up complexity up. I also recommend using the KISS principle when it comes to foraging as well.

As mentioned at the beginning of this chapter, there are at least 1000 edible plants to choose from in North America. We will not attempt to cover them all. There are way too many fish to chase at once. Instead we will concentrate on those wild edibles that are common, tasty, unique or have historic precedence for wide use. Also there are edible plants and there are edible plants. By this I mean some plants either discourage the harvesting of the edible parts or have dubious culinary qualities.

Eat With Seasons

Earth Peoples had no other choice than to eat with the seasons. Mankind has spent the vast majority of its existence as hunter-gatherers and thus, most of our evolution occurred with seasonal food gathering and ingestion. Many in the health food industry have argued that our bodies are predisposed to maximize significant health benefits by eating with the seasons. In any event, for the most part, we do not have any choice but to forage with the seasons, and almost all foods are proportionately better the fresher they are. Many of the plant identification books are either organized around the seasons or at least indicate which plant parts are edible in each season. The availability of many wild foods are very fleeting indeed, and if you miss them by one or two weeks they will be gone until next year without a trace. So go with the flow of nature and forage and eat with the seasons. Every month will bring new treasures.

Edible Wild Plants Foraging Guidelines

1. Never, ever eat a plant that has not been positively identified as edible. Make sure every detail is right.
2. Become familiar with poison look-alikes.
3. After positive identification, sample only a small amount the first time to avoid danger from allergic reactions or possible misidentification.
4. Always be sure the environment from which edible plants are collected is free of pollutants, including pesticides, herbicides, and high concentrations of fertilizers. Avoid power line easements, roadsides, railroad tracks, treated lawns, and agricultural runoff.
5. Never collect wild edibles near heavily traveled roads. Dangerous levels of heavy metals accumulate in plants from exhaust fumes and road sprays.
6. Before harvesting wild edible plants from public property; ensure collecting is allowed.
7. Always obtain permission before collecting wild edible plants from private property.
8. Always adopt the "caretaker" attitude while collecting wild edibles. Remember that this is Mother Nature's garden. Leave Nature better than you found it.
    a. Never collect all or most of any plant in an area.
    b. Never collect an endangered or rare plant.
    c. Re-seed and thin as necessary.
9. Avoid eating any raw wild edible plant that grows in standing water. They may contain Giardia or harmful bacteria.
10. Never, ever eat a plant that has not been positively identified as edible. Make sure every detail is right.

Chapter 2: The Big Ten

He causeth the grass to grow for the cattle and herbs for the service to man; that he may bring forth food out of the earth.

Psalm 104

Often I am asked to name some of the top wild edibles. Since I graduated from a Big Ten school, Purdue University, I picked what I call the Big Ten. These are wild food sources that can be found in abundance in almost every part of the country and in most cases the world. They include the Oaks; Pines; Grasses; Cattails; Dandelion; Opuntia; Lamb's-quarters; Nettles; Mustards; and Brambles, and Blueberries. I know that actually makes eleven. I will explain later.

The Big First: The Oaks

According to the New Grolier Multimedia Encyclopedia, 1993, there are over 450 Oak species, of which 60 are native to North America. The oaks (Quercus spp.) were an extremely important food source for Native Americans. In fact they were so important to the Pomo Indians of California they were their personal property that could be passed down through inheritance (Harris, 1971). They are still an extremely important food source for wildlife. Take note of the number of acorns on the ground in the fall. Some areas under oak trees will be literally carpeted with acorns. In the spring go back to the same spots that were previously covered and you will see very little left. These acorns did not just vanish into thin air; the squirrels, turkeys, deer, mice, and anything else that was able ate them. Acorns have also been extensively used to feed livestock.

The Oaks are divided into two main groups, the white oaks and the red oaks. The red oaks contain the so-called black oaks and the white oaks contain the bur oaks. One of the main discriminating features between the white oaks and the red oaks is that the latter have points on the end of their leaf lobes while white oaks are rounded and smooth. A mnemonic I use to keep them straight is, "The white man used round nosed bullets and the Indians used pointy arrows." I call it the cowboys and Indians mnemonic. The reason we want to distinguish between these two oak family groupings is that the red oaks contain significantly more tannic acid than the white oaks. This makes the white oak family the preferred food for both humans and animals. When given a choice, deer will always feed on white acorns first before eating the red ones. On the other hand the red oaks are preferable if you are trying to collect acorns for their higher tannic acid content. This may be the case for medicinal or utilitarian uses such as hide tanning.

The number one food product from the oak is the acorn. The acorn contains Calcium, Magnesium, Phosphorous, Potassium, 37% Fat, and 8% Protein (Harris, 1971). An acorn, often, is not edible due to the bitter quinine taste of tannic acid. Tannic acid can cause intestinal distress and death if consumed in large enough quantities. Some white oak acorns are said to be edible right out of their shells. That is, they are so "sweet," and low in tannic acid that leaching is not required. I have yet to find such an acorn. However, I did buy and plant two Idaho Bur Oak saplings, which were advertised to bare totally "sweet" acorns. Time will tell. In any event, unless you can find such acorns yourself, you must leach them. I suggest sticking to white oak acorns if available, because as mentioned previously, they have far less tannic acid to leach out.

Shelling

Shelling acorns is not a process I enjoyed until I came across a method used by Native Americans in northern California. They simply soak the acorns overnight, which causes them to split. Old women would shell the acorns. This method made it so easy to shell even the blind participated. Black Oaks were the favorites of these people (Murphey, 1990). Another method is to place the acorns near fire, toasting evenly until the outer shells become brittle. Rolling with a heavy rock could easily crack off the shells.

Leaching Tannic Acid from Acorns

One method of leaching tannic acid from acorns is the cold running water method. Place a quantity of shelled and smashed acorns in a cloth bag or clean sock then tie the bag of acorns into a fast running stream. Using this method it will take at least two to three days. Periodically check by tasting a sample of the acorns.

A second method of leaching acorns is the boiling water method. Place a quantity of shelled and smashed, chopped, or whole acorns in a large pan. Pour enough boiling water over them to fully cover. Do not grind finely using this method, as it will result in a sticky mush that will mostly stick to the pan. **Important: Do not place acorns in cold water and then boil, as this will fix the tannins. Only allow the acorns to come into contact with boiling water never warm or cold.** Start boiling a second pot of water. When this comes to a boil, pour the water off the acorns. <u>Save this tannic acid water. It has medicinal properties as an astringent for cuts, burns, scrapes and sores</u>. Pour the new boiling water over the acorns. Repeat until water comes out clear. This will usually take about two to three times.

A third method for removing tannins from acorns is the blender and refrigerator method as described by Suellen Ocean in her book *Acorns and Eat'em*. Place approximately one cup of acorns and three cups of water into a blender. Blend until the acorns are finely ground. Place blended mixture in the refrigerator and pour off stained water every day for about a week until the water remains clear.

A fourth method of leaching used by some Native Americans was to soak the acorns in a hot lye solution made from boiling water and wood ash. This would be followed by several washings in hot water as described in method two above (Harris, 1971).

Other Oak Foods

Other oak food products include flour, made from grinding the inner bark or cambium layer into flour. Never girdle a tree by stripping the bark all the way around the tree, this will disrupt the flow of sap and kill it. Take only small strips from the vertical axis of the tree. In any event, taking any bark from a tree will weaken it and allow insect and disease invaders easier access. The tiniest rootlets can be collected in a survival situation and cooked through several changes of water (Brown, 1985).

What to Do with Leached Acorns

Now that you have all these leached acorns, what can you do with them? The chopped, diced or whole products can be roasted in the oven on the fire. These may be salted, sweetened with honey, sugar, or brown sugar. Acorns can be substituted for any recipe calling for nuts or peanuts. The finely ground leached acorn meal can be used in breads and soups and porridge. You may substitute various amounts of acorn meal for flour in bread, pancakes, cornmeal, soups, stews, cakes, etc. Blueberries and maple syrup were often combined with acorn mush to make a tasty cereal (Harris, 1971). A great cookbook for acorns is a book called Acorns and Eat'em by Suellen Ocean (Ocean, 1985).

Acorn Nuts

The Big Second: The Pines

I can still remember to this day my childhood memories of Euell Gibbons advertising a breakfast cereal on television. During the commercial he points to a Pine Tree and says, "...did you know you can eat a pine tree, many parts are edible."

Pine Trees are evergreen cone bearing trees that have two to five leaves (needles), covered at the base by a papery sheath. An exception to this rule is the Single Leaf Piñon Pine which actually has two needles fused together. The cones are either the larger and more familiar female pinecones or the smaller male pollen cones. The three main foods from a pine tree are needles, nuts and pollen. All pine tree nuts, pollen and needles are edible.

Pine Needles

I was amazed years ago when I discovered the edibility of pine needles in the form of pine needle tea. Not only is this a pleasantly mild aromatic tea, but it delivers three to four times more vitamin C than fresh squeezed orange juice. The different species of pines have different flavors. Some have an orange flavor. The bright green new needles found in spring make the best tea, but Pine Needle tea can be made year round. The needles can also be picked and dried for later use. To make Pine Needle tea, gather enough needles to make about one tablespoon of chopped needles. Discard the turpentine-carrying sheath. Chop the needles and steep in very hot but not boiling water for about ten to fifteen minutes. Boiling water will destroy the Vitamin C and yield an unpleasant turpentine flavor. The other way I use pine needles is as trailside nibble. I'll grab a half a dozen or so pine leaves, pop them into my mouth and chew them until the flavor is gone. I also give myself an extra boost of vitamin C this way as an added bonus. Needles from the Eastern Hemlock trees and Firs can also be used.

Pine Pollen

Pine Pollen can be collected in the spring or early summer depending on the species and climate. The pollen is collected from the male cones or catkins by shaking the pollen filled cones into a bag. Pollen will only be available for about two weeks in any given area. Pollen can be used as a flour extender in breads, cakes, pancakes or anywhere wheat flour is used. This will add a unique flavor and enhance the nutritional value of any recipe.

Pine Nuts

Pine nuts are one of the crown jewels of wild edible foods. They have been harvested from the wild and cultivated forests for thousands of years in North America, Europe and Asia. All pine nuts are edible. Unfortunately not all pine trees were created equal when it comes to pine nut production. Some pine tree species produce only very small pine nuts. These trees are found mostly in eastern North America. These include the White, Virginia, Pitch and other long leaf varieties. The pine nuts on these are so small they hardly merit the effort of collection. Some of the pines in western North America that produce large pine nuts include Piñon, Coulter, Digger and Sugar species. Pine nuts from the Colorado Piñon and Single Leaf Piñon have been found to contain complete proteins, that is they contain all twenty amino acids required for a complete protein complement.

There is hope for those living east of the Mississippi to collect and process Pine Nuts fresh from the tree. There are several species of commercial cultivars used to produce pine nuts that are available from local and mail order nurseries. These include members of the stone pine group: Swiss Stone Pine, Korean Stone Pine and Italian Stone Pine. You may discover that the decorative pine tree in your yard or your neighbors' is one of these non-native producers of quality pine nuts.

To harvest and process pine nuts you must locate the pine trees before the pinecones open. Timing is everything in pine nut harvesting. You can either collect the unopened cones and heat them up near a fire or in your oven to release the nuts or you can wait for nature. In the latter case you must check the trees every day, as once they begin to fall, they will literally rain from the trees. Once they rain from the trees it will be a race between you and all of the creatures that find pine nuts as much of a delicacy as humans do. They will not lay around on the forest floor for long until they will all be gone. Once you have gathered a quantity of pine nuts they must be removed from their shells. The easiest way to do this is with heat. Place the pine nuts near a fire or in the oven long enough to make the shells brittle. Once the shells are brittle they can be easily cracked using a variety of methods.

Other evergreens

I generally don't like giving out rules for edibility in plants, because there are always exceptions that can result in deadly consequences. However, general rules are helpful in narrowing down identification or possible edibility in unknown plants. There are some general rules for the **evergreens** that protect them from being eaten by browsers such as deer in the winter. They protect themselves in one of three ways:

1. They are prickly or otherwise physically undesirable like the Pines or Holly.
2. They are hidden under leaves like Partridgeberry.
3. They are extremely toxic, like Mountain Laurel (CF, Vol X, No. 2).

These are general rules only. They are correct in most instances, however it doesn't account for all of the toxic possibilities, such as the lethal quantities of taxine found in American Yew seeds.

The Big Third: The Grasses

On 2 June 1995, while enforcing the no-fly zone over Bosnia, United States Air Force Captain Scott O'Grady's F-16 was shot down. For six days he evaded his enemy and survived on the bounty of the land. Among his dining fair were dirty water from his boots, ants, unspecified leaves, and grass. That is right, grass.

You are thinking that you can not eat grass. Only cows and horses can do that, right? Yes and no is the short answer. First let us dispense with the no side of the answer. You cannot run out to your front yard and begin to pull up handfuls of grass and begin eating it because of the high cellulose content. You simply will not be able to digest it. Even if you could bear to swallow the large mouthfuls of this fibrous material, you would eventually clog your digestive system and would probably die without medical intervention. Only animals with specially adapted digestive systems can convert the cellulose of grass into protein. Humans do not belong to this grazing club.

The Grass Family known as Gramineae has over 1300 distinct species. As domesticated humans we are familiar with several as primary food sources, including wheat, rice, corn, rye, sugar cane, barley, sorghum, millet, and oats. The first three of these, along with potatoes, constitute the majority of the food consumed on earth by humans (Facciola, 1990). When you also consider that the major food source for our domesticated grazing animals is also grass, this easily makes them the most important plant food source for mankind.

Of the hundreds of grass species, only a few are know to have any organic toxicity. Darnel (Lolium tamulentum) is reported to have poisonous or intoxicating seeds. Velvet Grass (Holcus lanatus) and Johnson Grass (Sorghum halenpense) leaves contain hydrocyanic acid. Bromus cathaticus and B. purgans may both cause stomach upset. (Fernald, 1958). Other references such as *100 Poisonous Plants of Maryland* report toxicity in Johnson Grass (Hill, 1985) as well. All of the other grasses are fair game.

How one goes about eating grass is probably your next question. The answer is there are several ways. One is to pull up some of the older leaves, chew, swallow the juices and spit out the cud. You can obtain significant nutritional benefits from the simple yet unappetizing method.

Nibble on the tender bases and joints of grasses of all ages as you may have done naturally as a child. Another method is to eat the very young sprouts that have not yet developed the undigestible fibers. There is a big market in the health food industry selling barley and wheat shoots juices as super-foods to keep you in top health. The adult leaves may also be dried and powdered using a blender, grain mill, mortar and pestle or mono matate (Native American mortal and pestle). This powder can be used as a healthful instant tea or flour extender (Fernald, 1958). The seeds are the most often sought after edible portion of the plant. Native Americans used these to make gruel and flours. The chaff must be removed from the seed by winnowing or parching.

A large member of the grass family, Reed (Phragmites communis) is most often referred to as Phragmites. It is a common wetland grass that grows up to 13 feet high. This plant is usually despised in America and desired in Europe. In America the plant is seen as an invasive pest that must be eradicated. In Europe it is seen as a valuable source of paper pulp and demand outstrips supply. In the United States the plant is studied for ways to eradicate it and in Europe it is studied to produce more. Phragmites is easily identified by its characteristic height and showy seed head that often finds its way into dried flower arrangements.

Collect the shoots in early spring and prepare like asparagus. Seeds can be collected from the mature seed heads and cooked, hull and all, into a nutritious gruel that was preferred by Native Americans. The rootstock was also collected and roasted or boiled like potatoes by Native Americans. Additionally the starch from within the roots can be scraped out with a knife and made into a paste with the addition of water. The paste is then set on a rock close to a fire where it will puff up into a marshmallow-like confection (Fernald, 1958).

The hollow reeds of the mature stems of Phragmites can be used as drinking straws, spiles for tree sap collection, quills for pens, stems for pipes, and blowing straws for making wooden utensils with coals.

Wild Rice (Zizania aquatica) is another prevalent wetland grass that was heavily dependent upon by Native Americans as a staple food. Like Phragmites this grass grows in similar environs. However, this grass is primarily used as a supplier of the superior grain, Wild Rice. The characteristic growth pattern of this plant makes it easy to spot from a distance. The seeds of this plant must be harvested at just the right time, as the slightest touch to ripe seeds will make them fall off. The seeds do not ripen all at once. These two characteristics of the Wild Rice plant are primarily responsible for its resistance to cultivation. However, it can be harvested in small quantities as the Native Americans have and continue to do so using a canoe with one paddler in the rear and a person up front to beat the seeds off into the canoe.

Any discussion on eating grasses is not complete without the inclusion of Ergot. Ergot is a disease of grasses and cultivated cereals caused by the fungus Claviceps purpurea and other members of the Genus Claviceps. As the species name implies the fungus is purplish in color. It can be found in the seed head where it replaces individual seeds with swollen purplish fungal masses that are shaped like the seeds.

Ergot has been responsible for much human death and suffering. As it contaminated cultivated fields of grain, particularly rye, it resulted in a disease known at the time as St Anthony's fire. It is known today as Ergotism. The onslaught of the disease would begin with fire-like pain in the limbs followed by gangrene, delirium, hallucinations and often death. Often these symptoms were viewed as proof of demonic possession or witchcraft, which carried with it other undesirable side effects from your neighbors.

Ergot is the source of many drugs including LSD-25 (lysergic acid diethylamide), Ergotamine - a migraine treatment, and Ergotoxine used to stop uterine bleeding. Considering the LSD connection it is not surprising to see the symptoms associated with ingestion of ergot. Today ergot is intentionally cultivated for drug production. Always inspect all grains for the presence of this deadly toxic agent.

Author standing in front of **Phragmites**

Wild Rice

The Big Fourth: Cattails

I can think of no other North American plant that is more useful than the cattail. This wonderful plant is a virtual gold mine of survival utility. It is a four-season food, medicinal and utility plant. What other plant can boast eight food products, three medicinals, and at least twelve other functional uses?

The Common Cattail (Typha latifolia) and its brethren Narrowleaf Cattail (Typha angustifolia), Southern Cattail (Typha domingensis), and Blue Cattail (Typha glauca) have representatives found in North America and most of the world. While living in Northern Japan, I spent many chilling mornings in snowstorms among miles of cattails while duck hunting. Just about any place you can find year round standing water or wet soil you can usually find cattails.

In Euell Gibbons' *Stalking the Wild Asparagus*, his chapter on cattails is titled "Supermarket of the Swamp." As you will see this title aptly applies to cattail. However, due to its medicinal and utilitarian uses we may want to mentally modify the title to "Super Wal-Mart of the Swamp."

The characteristic brown seed head readily identifies cattails. However there are some poisonous look-alikes that may be mistaken for cattail. None of these look alikes possess the brown seed head. Blue Flag (Iris versicolor) and Yellow Flag (Iris pseudoacorus) and other members of the iris family all posses the cattail like leaves but none possesses the brown seed head. All members of the Iris family are poisonous. Another look alike which is not poisonous, but whose leaves look more like cattail than Iris, is the Sweetflag (Acorus calamus). Sweetflag has a very pleasant spicy sweet aroma when the leaves are bruised. It also does not possess the brown seed head. Sweetflag and Iris are more flat at their bases and are splayed out like a hand of playing cards. Day-lilies also grow in this splayed playing card fashion. Sedges have a central raised ridge in the center of their leaves. Neither the Irises nor Cattail have the sweet spicy aroma possessed by the Sweetflag. I have seen large stands of Cattails and Sweetflag and Irises growing side by side. As with all wild edibles, positive identification is essential. If you are not sure do not eat it.

In just about any survival situation whether self imposed or not, one of the first plants I will look for is the cattail. As a food plant, cattails are outstanding and offer a variety of food products according to the season. In winter and early spring dig up the roots to locate the small pointed shoots called corms. These can be removed, peeled and eaten fresh, added with other spring greens for a salad, or cooked in stews or alone as a potherb. Be advised that eating any **raw** aquatic plant present the risk of contracting Giardia. As the plant growth progresses where the shoots reach a height of two to three feet above the water, peel and eat like the corms or sauté. This food product is also known as "Cossack Asparagus" due to the Russians fondness for it (Gibbons, 1962).

In late spring to early summer, some of my favorite food products come into fruition on the cattail. Soon after these shoots become available, the green female bloom spikes and the male pollen spikes begin to emerge. These spikes can be found in the center of the plant and form a cylindrical projection that can only be detected while close to the plant. Peel back the leaves in the same way you would shuck corn and both the male portion above and the female below can be seen. The female portion will later develop into the familiar brown "cattail" seed head from which the plant's name is derived. The male portion will atrophy into a small dried twig that may easily break off the top of the seed head. Both the male and female pollen spikes can be boiled and eaten like corn on the cob and are both delicious. The male portion provides a bigger meal at this stage. They have a flavor that is corn-like, but distinct from corn. I cannot imagine anyone finding the flavor objectionable. Both may also be eaten raw. The risk of contracting Giardia from these portions of the plant is minimal due to their physical separation from the water.

Later the male pollen head will begin to develop an abundance of yellow pollen with a talcum powder consistency that can easily be shaken off into any container. Several pounds of this can be collected in less than an hour. The traditional use of this pollen is to substitute for some of the flour in pancakes to make cattail pancakes. This also works well with cornbread. Other uses of the pollen include thickeners or flour extenders for breads, cakes, etc.

In late summer to early fall the inner tender portions of the leafstalk may still be collected, but the availability of this Cossack Asparagus begins to dwindle due to the toughening up of the plant. During this period and all the way to spring, the most abundant food product, the root starch, may be harvested. It is so abundant, a study was conducted at the Cattail Research Center of Syracuse University's department of plant sciences. The chief Investigator of the project was Leland Marsh. The results as they reported were as follows:

"Yields are fantastic. Marsh discovered he could harvest 140 tons of rhizomes per acre near Wolcott, NY. That represents something more than 10 times the average yield per acre of potatoes. In terms of dry weight of cattail flour, the 140 tons of roots would yield approximately 32 tons." (Harris, 1971)

To extract the flour or starch from the cattail root, simply collect the roots, wash and peel them. Next break up the roots under water and the flour will begin to separate from the fibers. Continue this process until fibers are separated and the sweet flour is removed. Remove the fiber and pour off the excess water and allow the remaining flour slurry to dry by placing near a fire or in the sun. Cattail root flour also contains gluten. Gluten is the constituent in wheat flour required allowing flour to rise in yeast breads. Additionally, the Iroquois Indians macerated and boiled the roots to produce a fine syrup, which they used in a corn meal pudding and to sweeten other dishes (Murphey, 1990). Some Indians burned the mature brown seed heads to extract the small seeds from the fluff, which was used to make gruel and added to soup.

The medicinal uses of cattails include poultices made from the split and bruised roots that can be applied to cuts, wounds, burns, stings, and bruises. The ash of the burned cattail leaves can be used as an antiseptic or styptic for wounds. A small drop of a honey-like excretion can often be found near the base of the plant that can be used as an antiseptic for small wounds and toothaches.

The utility of cattail is only limited to your imagination. The dried stalks can be used for hand drills and arrow shafts. The seed heads and dried leaves can be used as tinder. The seed head fluff can be used for pillow and bedding stuffing or as a down in clothing. The leaves can be used for construction of shelters, woven seats and backs of chairs, which has been a traditional use for hundreds of years. They can be woven into baskets, hats, mats, and beds. The dried seed heads attached to their stalks can be dipped into melted animal fat or oil and used as torches. The next time you see The Super Wal-Mart of the Swamp why not do some shopping?

Collecting Cattails

Examining Cossack Asparagus

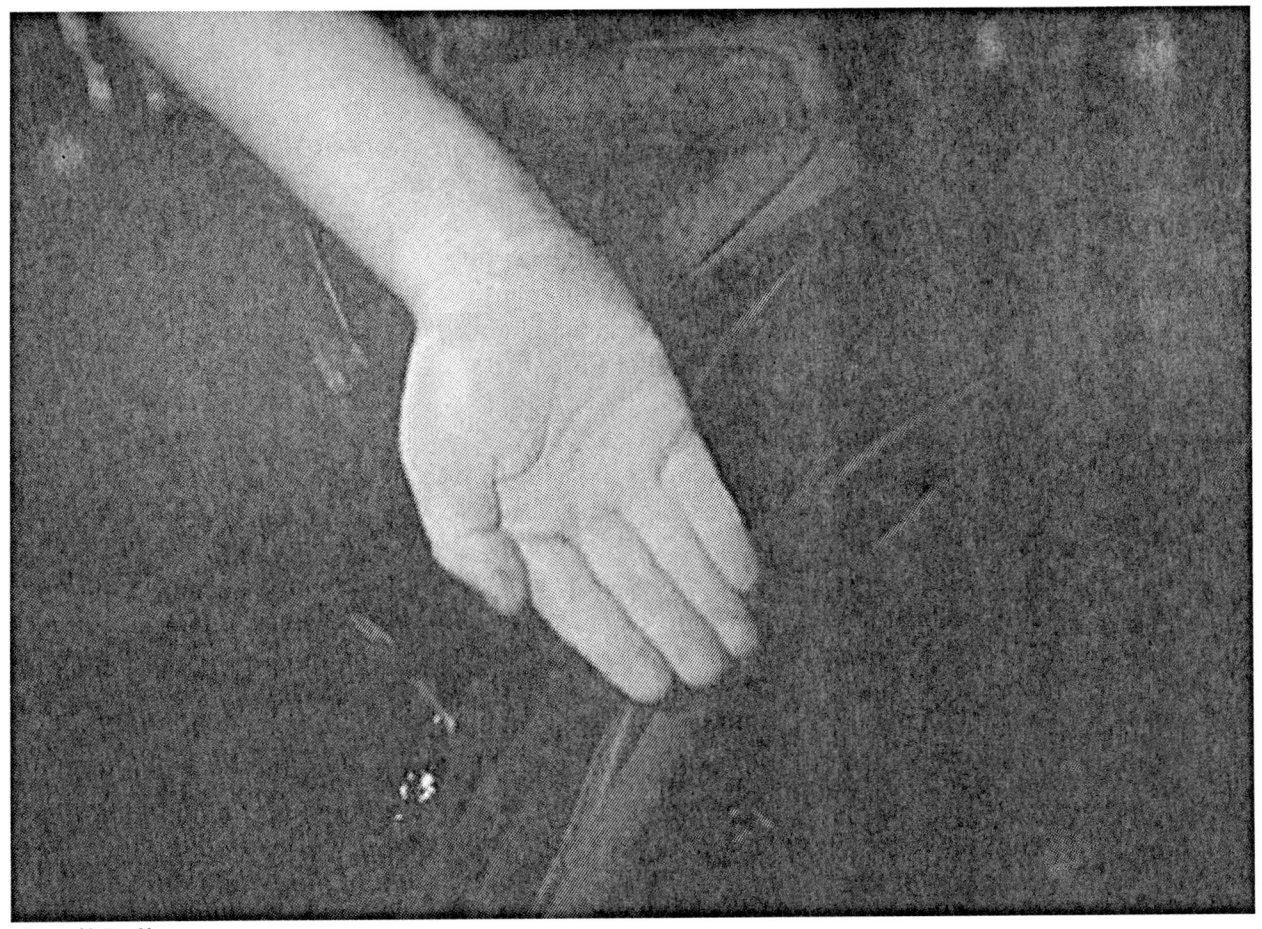

Cattail Pollen

The Big Fifth: Dandelion

I have seen them in Japan, Korea, Hong Kong, Australia, Great Britain, and Europe as well as in my own back yard. They are ubiquitous. Europeans brought dandelions (Taraxacum offinale) to this country originally as food and a medicine plant. With their highly mobile parachute seed heads that are carried by the wind they quickly spread across the continent. They are persistently targeted by the herbicide and lawn care industry as public enemy number one. This is just a perception or point of view error. They are only undesirable because like in the case of most weeds, people do not understand what a treasure they are. Dandelions are a choice edible, whether you collect them from your own chemical free lawn or some other safe environment. Do not poison your dandelions, cultivate and eat them.

Every part of the Dandelion is edible except for the flower stalk and the bracts below the flower. The flower stalk contains milky latex–like substance that is very unpalatable and the bracts are extremely bitter. The leaves are best harvested before the flower buds appear, as they become very strong in flavor and bitter afterwards. Once the plant is no longer flowering the leaves are once again less bitter. They can be added to salads raw or cooked as a green. The flowers are edible raw and can be added to salads. They are slightly sweet and gummy in texture. They can also be made into fritters, but be sure to remove most of the bract before cooking. It is not necessary to remove the entire bract as a little will not make the flower too bitter. The flowers can also be used to make a tea known as Dandelion Shrub. It will have a very eye pleasing yellow color and be mellow taste. Between the roots of the plant and the leaves is a white central part of the plant known as the crown. The crowns are most often prepared as fritters, but may also be eaten raw or added to soups and stews. The root itself may be boiled or eaten raw as vegetable. Make a coffee substitute by roasting and grinding the root. I do not think it tastes too much like coffee, but it is a very healthful herb beverage.

The Dandelion is more nutritious than any vegetable you can typically buy in the grocery store. See the section on Nutrition Enhancers in the chapter on Wilderness Medicine for a rundown. The Dandelion is truly a super-food.

Many towns hold annual Dandelion Festivals in the United States and Canada to honor the virtues of this incredible edible. Vineland, New Jersey is the self proclaimed Dandelion capital of the world. There is an entire book dedicated to this herb called *The Dandelion Celebration* by Peter Gail. This book is a wealth of information about the Dandelions including history, folklore, nutrition, and over 75 recipes. The next time you take a walk in your back yard, look to see if your lawn is blessed with this magnificent plant.

Dandelion

The Big Sixth: Prickly Pear Cactus

I first encountered Prickly Pear Cactus (Opuntia humifusa) as a teenager in southern Indiana. I could not believe that cactus grew in Indiana, but there it was on a dry rocky outcropping in great abundance. I collected a small amount and transplanted them to a dry area in my backyard, where they flourished for years. My next experience with Prickly Pear Cactus was at Eglin Air Force base in Fort Walton Beach, Florida, where I was attending Survival school as part of my Naval Flight Training. During this survival training, the Prickly Pear Cactus and Saw Palmetto (Serenoa repens) were our two primary food sources. Whereas the Saw Palmetto provided a small tender nibble after much wrestling with the tough plant, the Prickly Pear Cactus provided a much easier harvest. This species of Prickly Pear had fairly large tubers that were collected in large quantities and provided the base of our evening meals. They tasted very similar to potatoes after cooking.

Several years later I discovered the other virtues of this wonderful plant including the edible prickly pears that are often made into jams and jellies. Although the eastern species fruits do not get as large as those do in the west, they are edible. The pads or leaves of the Prickly Pear can also be eaten. Remove the large thorns and the smaller fine red hair thorns. These smaller thorns or best removed by parching or wiping with a damp cloth. I remember an occasion during my survival training when I removed these smaller red thorns from the roof of the mouth and tongue of a shipmate who had been a little careless about their removal prior to eating. While the experience was educational for me, it was extremely educational and painful for my friend. The pads can be skinned or not before boiling or added to soups or stews. They will be mucilaginous in character when cooked and like okra, will thicken soups and stews. If desired, boil them in a change of water to eliminate some of the slimy character. The seeds can also be parched, ground into flour, and used as a thickener.

The split raw pads can be used fleshy side down as a poultice for cuts, burns, and bruises. Also the raw pads are a great source of fresh water as cactus are over 90% water.

Prickly Pear Cactus

The Big Seventh: Lamb's-quarters

Lamb's-quarters (Chenopodium album) also known as Goosefoot is a common weed in disturbed areas, lawns and gardens. It is also an indicator plant for healthy soil. This hearty annual produces large multi-branched plants that yield tens of thousands of seeds per plant. Its goose foot-shaped leaves easily identify this plant with a characteristic mealy white coating on the underside of the leaves and on the top new leaves. Once you have made an acquaintance with Lamb's-quarters, it is easily recognizable even at a distance by its characteristic growth pattern. Collect the tender new growth throughout the year.

Lamb's-quarters is a delicious wild edible. It reminds me of mild spinach. It is one of the most nutritious foods you can eat as well (see section on Nutrition Enhancers). Everyone in my family, including my sometimes-picky children will eat Lamb's-quarters, but not spinach. It may be steamed in it own juices for ten minutes, but will be greatly reduce in volume. Use in any recipe calling for spinach such as spinach and feta cheese pies. One of our favorite recipes is to quickly sauté steamed Lamb's-quarters in olive oil and fresh chopped garlic. Squeeze fresh lemon juice over the Lamb's-quarters before serving and salt and pepper to taste.

The Peruvian ancestors of the Incas cultivated the popular health food grain quinoa. It has been promoted in this country as a super-food and as a price to match its status. Quinoa (Chenopodium quinoa) is from the same genus as Lamb's-quarters and a very close relative. The seeds of Lamb's-quarters can be used likewise. Just think of Lamb's-quarters as free North American quinoa. Your time is the only investment you need to acquire it. After collecting the seeds, dry and grind them to make nutritious flour. The seeds can also be used whole as for hot cereal or to add to cakes and breads.

If all this super-food status isn't enough, then use the roots as a soap substitute, as they are rich in sapponins. Sapponins are naturally occurring phytochemicals in some plants that act like soap.

Two cautions are in order about Lamb's-quarters. One is that they contain oxalic acid as do spinach and beet greens, and should not be eaten on a daily basis as they may inhibit absorption of calcium. This calcium-blocking phenomenon is just as likely to occur from spinach, beets and other members of the spinach family. Lamb's-quarters may also absorb too many nitrates in certain locales, particularly near farm fields where large amounts of synthetic fertilizers may accumulate and be absorbed by the plant. This has resulted in nitrate poisoning in livestock while overgrazing on Lambs-quarters.

Lamb's-Quarters

The Big Eighth: Nettles

I have many memories as a child running through thickets of Wood Nettles (Laportea canadensis) at the edge of the forest. Wood Nettles have tiny stinging hairs that inject formic acid when they rub against your skin, resulting in welts much like those encountered from ant bites. Although handling plants must be done with finesse, it is well worth the effort. Other members of the Nettle family include Stinging Nettle (Utrica dioica) and Slender Nettle (Utrica gracilis). The young tender leaves of all three of these plants make a highly nutritious and delicious potherb and tea. For best results cook these greens in a pot without the addition of water for best results. Their own juices will provide the liquid and cook until just tender. Do not overcook. These plants contain more protein than any known leafy vegetable as well as ample amounts of vitamins A and C, and Iron. Using gloves to harvest leaves or harvesting from the top will reduce stings. Immediately rub Jewelweed (Impatiens spp.) or Curled Dock (Rumex crispus) on the stings to reduce pain and swelling. Both plants are edible as potherbs as well.

Another popular way to prepare Nettles is Nettle Soup. Nettle soup is usually prepared by sauteing onions (wild or otherwise) and celery in butter until tender, add flour to thicken followed with chicken stock and cream to further thicken. Add lots of Nettles and simmer for twenty minutes. Pine nuts may be added upon serving.

Stinging Nettle

The Big Ninth: Mustards

The Mustard family has produced much of our domesticated produce. All vegetables belonging to the cruciferae family known as the crucifix vegetables include horseradish, cresses, cabbage, broccoli, cauliflower, turnips, kale, kohlrabi, radish, and of course the mustards all came from the wild mustard family. The most common wild mustards include the woodlands loving Wintercress (Barbarea vulgaris), Garlic Mustard (Allaria esculenta), Field Mustard (Brassica rapa), and Black Mustard (Brassica nigra). All of the mustards can be used as highly nutritious greens particularly from the young new basal growth. The older growth becomes tough and too bitter to eat. The seeds can be collected, mashed, and mixed with vinegar and oil to make the condiment mustard. The seeds can also be used as a pepper substitute, with just the right hotness.

Euell Gibbons frequently wrote about Wintercress, which is also known as Yellow Rocket about. This plant is one of the earliest plants to appearing in the growing season. In fact it doesn't even come close to waiting until spring. It appears in winter sometimes in January or February. The young tender growth should be eaten raw or cooked before the flower buds appear. The raw leaves have a unique pungent flavor. Once the buds appear, the leaves become too bitter to eat raw. The buds and leaves may be eaten at this time by cooking in two changes of water. Adding baking soda to the water may also help reduce the bitterness. This is a case of the early bird gets the worm, because if you wait too long in the winter you will see nothing but the older flowering plants.

Garlic Mustard is an introduced European species that prefers woodlands. It is rapidly out-competing native woodland plant species. This plant has a garlic flavor, and should be harvested with reckless abandon, as it seems to have nothing else holding it in check. Some states such as Indiana have organized Garlic Mustard pulls to try to eradicate this invader. The roots of this plant can also be used as a horseradish substitute, or a great vegetable.

Field Mustard, also known as Rape and Black Mustard are often seen growing in open fields. Their showy yellow flowers easily identify both. Another cultivated species of Mustard also is known as Rape and is the source of canola oil.

A Bowl of cooked mustard

The Big Tenth: Berries: Brambles and Blueberries

You may have noticed that I cheated on number ten and grouped two different plant families together. As I was formulating this list, both groups of plants were competing for the position. I soon realized they naturally gravitated together in my mind because they tend to group together in nature. Usually when I enter a hardwood forest woods one or both of these plant families will have representatives easily available.

Brambles

Gray's Manual of Botany lists 205 different species of Brambles (Rubus spp. or Rhubus spp.). All are non-climbing and most are bristly shrubs with five white petaled flowers. They all bear juicy red or black multi-segmented berries. There are basically three major subgroups; Raspberries, Blackberries, and Dewberries. Raspberries have a bloom or white powder covering their *round* stemmed canes with black or red berries that are hollowed once picked blackberries. Blackberries are tall arching *angular* stemmed canes. Dewberries are *short flattened* shrubs less than one foot tall with *trailing stems* and blackberry-like berries.

The fruits can be eaten raw or used for jellies, jam, juices, and wines. Teas can be made from the tender leaves. The tender *Blackberry* shoots can be eaten raw. What a great group of plants!

There are two major cautions when collecting Bramble products. The first is the vicious thorns that are not shy about revealing their presence. These thorns are very tough and can easily tear cloth and flesh alike before breaking. The second threat, chiggers, which are subtler initially, but are much more detrimental in the long run. These eight-legged members of the mite family are not insects. They are close relatives of ticks, but are smaller than deer ticks. There are fifty species that attack man. They prefer to bite where clothing is tight fitting like the waist. The bite itself is not painful but the aftermath results in severe itching for days at the bite sight. Before collecting brambles or other berries Use herbal bug repellents such as Pennyroyal or Mountain Mint. Apply particularly heavily where the clothing fits tightly, like at the waistline and under socks. It is rare that I have found brambles with berries that were not infested with chiggers. Forewarned is forearmed.

Blueberries

Blueberries (Vaccinium spp.) are always a treat to find in the wild. They are usually smaller than domestic ones, but their flavor is more concentrated. There are many different individual species and are often difficult to tell one from the other, but they all are excellent eating. As in brambles the biggest threat to collecting Blueberries can be chiggers. On a recent outing in Maryland my family and I went on a Blueberry and Huckleberry (Gaylussacia spp.) picking foray. We were late by about a week for the peak of the harvest and the birds and other animals had nearly stripped the bushes clean. However, the chiggers were there in force and we collected more irritating chiggers than we did berries. We had all neglected to apply herbal bug repellents, so we were at their mercy. We all learned a valuable lesson that day that will not be soon forgotten. Do not forget the bug spray.

The Huckleberries look very similar to Blueberries and have a similar taste. Most people would probably think they were Blueberries. They are closely related but from a different genus. There are several differences between the two groups of plants. They both have small elliptical leaves, but the Huckleberry leaves are a little bit more textured or bubbly. They both have the familiar five-pointed calyx crown on the berry, but the Huckleberry calyx does not protrude out like the Blueberry. The biggest and most unmistakable difference is that the Blueberry has numerous small soft seeds that are not noticed when eating. The Huckleberry has exactly ten large crunchy seeds that can be felt crunching while chewing the berry. The bottom line is that they are both delicious and fun to pick.

Blueberry

Chapter 3: Aquatic Wild Edibles

"And God said Behold, I have given you every herb bearing seed, which is upon the face of all the earth, and every tree, in which is the fruit of a tree yielding seed; to you shall be meat. "

Genesis 1:29

When searching for wild edibles, I am always drawn to water. I know that there will usually be an abundance of edible wild plants nearby in these transition areas. Transition areas are natural areas where two different biomes meet like field meets woods, water meets field, water meets woods, etc. These areas are richer in biodiversity than either of the adjoining areas making up the transition. The water to woods and water to field transition areas are particularly rich.

Mints

Besides choice aquatic edible plants, a selection of land loving edible plants that appreciate a steady supply of water from the moist soil may also be present. Some of these include members of the Labiatae or Mint family such as Peppermint (Mentha piperita) and Spearmint (Mentha spicata). There are over 600 members of the Mentha genus along. Gray's Manual of Botany lists 39 genera in the Mint family. As you can see this is a huge family of plants. One characteristic that most mints share in common is that they possess a square stem. However, not all plants that have a square stem are mints, but most are.

Chufa

Look for Yellow Nut Grass or Chufa (Cyperus esculentus) near the water's edge. This is really not a grass but a member of the Sedge family, which is often characterized by its three sided leaves. The many small tubers found growing on the end of their roots can be eaten raw or cooked. The tubers of groundnut grow at the end long fragile roots. Therefore, do not pull the plant from the ground and expect to collect the tubers, they will break off and be left in the ground. Dig deep and wide to get to these hidden treasures.

Groundnut

One of my favorite wild edibles, Groundnut (Apios americana), is often found near the edge of the water, as it is a moisture loving plant. This member of the pea family possesses many pea-like characteristics including brown or lavender pea-like flowers, weak stemmed twining vines, green-bean like seeds and peanut-like tubers the size of walnuts strung along its roots.

Boil the tubers in heavily salted water and eat while still hot for a delicious treat. The groundnuts become significantly less palatable when cold. They have a taste similar to boiled peanuts for those familiar with this Southern treat. The seeds found in the seed pods can be used like lentils.

Members of the bramble family including Blackberry (Rubus allegheniensis) and Black Raspberries (Rubus occidentalis) frequently are found near water. Blueberries (Vaccinium corymbosum) and Cranberries (Vaccinium macrocarpon) can also be found particularly in acidic soils that are often indicated by the predominance of pine trees. Willows (Salix spp.) grow along as well as in the water. These plants are primarily known for their salicin content that can be used similar to aspirin. This water-loving tree is also very useful in making willow baskets and other items.

"Digging one day for fishworms, I discovered the groundnut (Apios tuberosa) on its string, the potato of the aborigines, a sort of fabulous fruit, which I had begun to doubt if I had ever dug and eaten in childhood, as I had told, and had not dreamed it. I had often since seen its crumpled red velvety blossom supported by the stems of other plants without knowing it to be the same. Cultivation has well-nigh exterminated it. It has a sweetish taste, much like that of a frost-bitten potato, and I found it better boiled than roasted. This tuber seemed like a faint promise of Nature to rear her own children and feed them simply here at some future period. In these days of fatted cattle and waving grain-fields this humble root, which was once the totem of an Indian tribe, is quite forgotten, or known only by its flowering vine; but let wild Nature reign here once more, and the tender and luxurious English grains will probably disappear before a myriad of foes, and without the care of man the crow may carry back even the last seed of corn to the great cornfield of the Indian's God in the southwest, whence he is said to have brought it; but the now almost exterminated ground-nut will perhaps revive and flourish in spite of frosts and wildness, prove itself indigenous, and resume its ancient importance and dignity as the diet of the hunter tribe."

Henry David Thoreau

Groundnut

Sweetflag

As you expand your search into the water, you may find other desirable edible plants. These include Cattail (Typha latifolia) with its multiple edible parts and Sweetflag (Acorus calamus) with its aromatic root that can be used to make candy. Make Sweetflag candy by boiling small chopped sections of the roots in several changes of boiling water and then rolling in sugar and dry. Be extremely careful not to confuse the aromatic Sweetflag and the familiar seed head bearing Cattail with the extremely poisonous members of the iris family including Blue Flag (Iris versicolor) and Yellow Flag (Iris pseudoacorus). The water is where you may find the most poisonous plant in North America, Water Hemlock (Cicuta maculata). Water Hemlock is a member of the carrot family that sports multiple parsnip-like roots. Ingesting only small amounts of this deadly plant may result in an extremely painful and gruesome death. Although this plant may be hard to confuse with other aquatic plants it does bear a resemblance to other members of the carrot family. These include the edible Wild Carrot (Daucus carota) and Poison Hemlock (Conium macullatum) that Socrates used to take his own life. Become familiar with these poisonous plants and always ensure positive identification by using reliable identification guides. If you are not positive, do not take any chances.

American Lotus

Other choice edible plants to look for in aquatic environments include American Lotus (Nelumbo lutea), Arrowhead (Sagittaria spp.), and Watercress (Nasturtium officinale). American Lotus may be easily confused with Spatterdock (Nuphar advena) or Bullhead-Lily (Nuphar variegatum). Both of the latter plants are edible, but are not as palatable. Watershield (Brasenia schreberi) is a member of the same family as American Lotus. Watershield has smaller elliptical floating leaves. The young leaves of Watershield can be cooked like greens (McPherson, 1977). Phragmites or Reed root can also be harvested and boiled for a winter vegetable. They also do not grow the extremely long roots with large starch rich tubers. American Lotus is also noteworthy as a possible mushroom poisoning antidote. Young American Lotus leaves may be eaten along with their seeds. Look up these three plants in a reliable identification guide and their differences will become readily apparent.

American Lotus

Arrowhead

Arrowhead can be easily confused with poisonous Arrow Arum (Peltandra virginica) or the edible Pickerelweed (Pontederia cordata). Arrowhead leaves are highly variable in shape. Sometimes the leaf will have the classic arrowhead shape with the two tails and sometimes they are oval. Veins radiating from the base of the leave identify arrowhead. The Slender Arrowhead has almost grasslike leaves. Arrow Arum contains the same caustic compound, oxalate acid crystals found in Jack-in-the-Pulpit (Arisaema atrorubens) and other related plants. Eating this plant may result in an experience described as eating a handful of wasps in which the tongue and throat feel as if they are receiving continuous stings. The throat can also swell, causing choking and possible strangulation.

Arrow Arum has pinnate veins while Arrowhead and Pickerelweed leaves veins are palmate. Parallel veins all originate from a central vein running the length of the leaf. Palmate veins originate from the base of the leaf as your fingers originate from the base of your hand. Arrowhead is also known as duck potato or by its Indian name Wapato. Native women gathered these tubers in the cold autumn waters by dislodging them from the bottom with their toes. The duck potatoes would then float to the surface where they could be easily plucked from the water. Pickerelweed seeds can be eaten like nuts and young tender leaf stocks can be used in salads or boiled as a potherb. Again, be sure to avoid the caustic Arrow Arum.

Caustic Arrow Arum on left and edible Arrowhead on right

Reed

Another water loving plant is Phragmites or Reed (Phragmites communis) which can be found growing near the water's edge. This giant grass is distinguished by its plume-like flower head. Young shoots and leaves can be eaten raw or cooked. The roots are available year-round and can be prepared as in cattail. Seeds can be used in gruels as in most grasses.

Great Bulrush

Great Bulrush (Scirpus validus) can be found in similar environments as Cattails and Wild Rice. Bulrush has many edible parts, including young tender shoots, pollen, ripe seeds and tender roots. Starch can be gathered from the older roots as in Cattail, by breaking up roots in a container of water. The starch or flour will fall to the bottom of the container. Pour off the excess water and collect the wet flour from the bottom. Dry and store in closed containers. This flour can be used in breads, as a soup thickener, or in any other way in which to use flour.

Wild Rice

Wild Rice (Zizania aquatica) which is a familiar grocery store item can be found in marshes, ponds and streams, both fresh and brackish. Harvesters used canoes in the traditional Native

American harvest technique. They canoed into the Wild Rice, bent the seed heads over their boats and batted the ripe seeds into their boats with sticks. The harvesting period for wild rice is only a few short days, as the seeds will easily fall from the plants when ripe.

Duckweed

Duckweed (Spirodela polyrhiza) is a very small aquatic plant sometimes found in great abundance. From a distance it appears as algae covering a pond. Upon closer inspection you may discover that the green algae is actually thousands of small individual 3/16" diameter oval plants known as Duckweed. This unusual plant can be added whole to soups or stews.

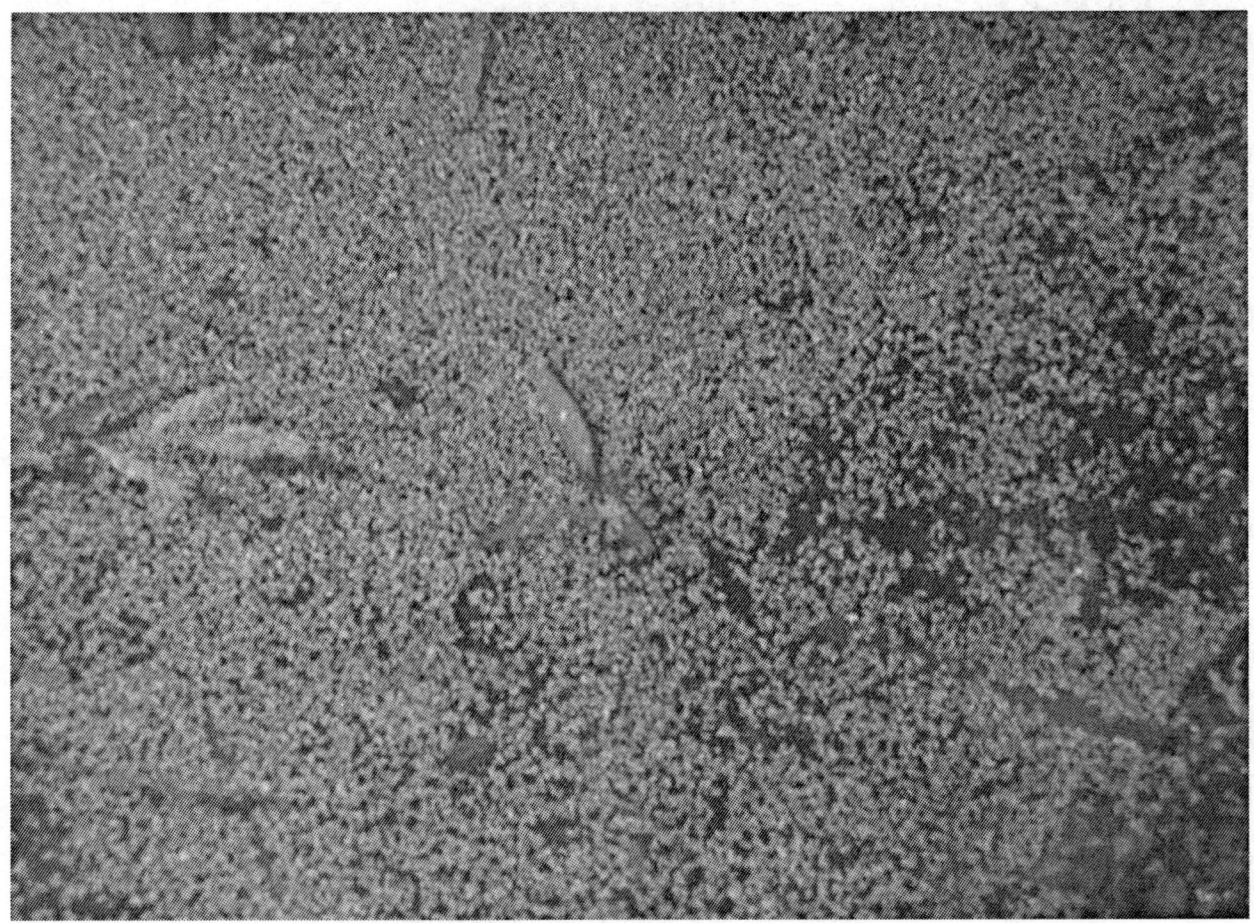

Duckweed

Water Purity

Another special caution when dealing with edible wild plants from aquatic environments is to ensure the water source is pure. This includes agricultural runoff that can be as bad or worse than some industrial pollutants. Also, all plant materials taken from open water sources, even in the purest of environments should be cooked. This will alleviate the possibility of Giardia that can be carried by wild animals that frequent the water. Alaska, which is one of the purest ecosystems in the world, is notorious for a high Giardia count due to the abundance of ungulates, including Mule Deer, Moose, Caribou, and Elk.

Remember that positive identification of plants is essential. Allergic reactions can occur whenever a new plant is eaten, either domestic or wild. Sample new foods sparingly at first, as allergic reactions can turn deadly. If you are not absolutely sure, do not take a chance. Bon appetit!

Chapter 4: Wet Forest Edibles

There is in every American, I think, something of the Old Daniel Boone–who, when he could see the smoke from another chimney, felt himself too crowded and moved further out into the wilderness.

Hubert H. Humphrey

There is nothing more inviting in the wilderness experience than a trek through a large hardwood forest. These forests are usually visually limited by their lack of light penetration, density and terrain. I think this is a key to their allure. The unexpected or hoped for can be just around the next bend or over the next hill. My young son best illustrates this allure, when he speaks of hiking on the Adventure Trail in the southern Indiana's Harrison-Crawford Forestry. The excitement in his voice and twinkle in his eyes conjures up all his boyhood fantasies of the wilderness experience. While hiking in a hardwood forest, we always take the opportunity to partake of some of the fine foraging.

The hardwood forest consists of a predominant mix of deciduous trees, often accompanied by stands or a scattering of conifers. Hardwood forests are predominantly wet or dry. In a wet hardwood forest the forest floor is usually wet even during prolonged dry spells. Burrowing your hands under the debris after a significant period of no precipitation in a wet hardwood forest reveals significant moisture. A wet hardwood forest will generally maintain a cool moist floor year round. Often there may be pools of standing water even during short periods of drought. Other good signs of wet hardwood forest are indicator plants including Mayapple (Podophyllum peltatum), Jack-in-the-Pulpit (Arisaema triphyllum), Black Cohosh (Cimicifuga racemosa) and others. There are many more wild edibles available in the wet hardwood forest than those mentioned in this chapter. Some of the more notable are presented here.

Year-round

I make my favorite tea from the small roots of the Sassafras (Sassafras albidum) which is available year round. This was an original ingredient in root beer. Recent studies have shown a main constituent of sassafras, safrole, to be carcinogenic (CF, Vol 6, Num 6). However, another recent study on the relative risk of various carcinogens suggests one beer has twelve times the risk as one cup of sassafras tea (Ames, 1987). I do not drink alcohol, but I will continue to drink sassafras tea. Gumbo File' is the Cajun seasoning and thickener made from the dried and crushed young spring and summer leaves of the sassafras.

The young leaves, twigs, and bark of the Spicebush (Lindera benzoin), make another delightful year-round tea. The fire engine red berries make a great allspice substitute by pitting, drying and crushing into a powder.

A prince of wild edibles, the Groundnut (Apios americana) can also be found year round in the wet hardwood forest. Found mostly around ravines and streams, the Groundnut provides strings of sweet turnip-like tubers that were once a major trade item of Native Americans. These should be eaten while hot as the flavor deteriorates rapidly as they cool. Roast the pods to separate beans from pod and then oil, salt and roast beans as you would for peanuts or use like lentils.

Sassafras

Spicebush

Wild Grapes (Vitis spp.) are in the Vitaceae or Grape Family and have many individual species, all of which are equally edible. The new tendrils are edible and may be eaten as a trail nibble or added to salads. The new young leaves are edible raw or cooked. They may be blanched in boiling water for 5 minutes to be used in traditional stuffed grape leaf recipes. They may also be canned in salted water for later use. The grapes are also edible and vary in flavor from very sour to sweet. All grapes contain natural pectin and are excellent for making jams, jellies, juice and wine. Grapes can be dried under the windshield of your car for raisins as well.

There are two other vines that may be mistaken for Grapes; Poison Ivy and deadly Canadian Moonseed. Poison Ivy does not really look like the grape, as Poison Ivy leaves grow in a pattern of three and they are not heart-shaped. Poison Ivy also uses lateral red hairs to attach itself closely to trees. Nonetheless if grapevines are growing in a woods then there is probably Poison Ivy growing there as well, often intertwined together. Grapevines are loose hanging vines that attach themselves with their tendrils. Canadian Moonseed (Menispermum canadense) does look more similar to Grape but is rarer than both Grape and Poison Ivy. It does not have tendrils so it tends to wind itself around a tree for support. It does have heart shaped leaves like the grape and bears a deadly fruit that resembles the grape as well. There are several distinguishing differences as the following chart illustrates:

	Grape	**Moonseed**
Leaves	Heart Shaped, toothed	Heart Shaped, untoothed
Seeds	More than one, roundish	One, flat crescent shaped
Support	Uses tendrils	No tendrils, winds around tree

Spring and Early Summer

The spring provides a plethora of foraging in the wet hardwood forest. You will not have to walk far to encounter Briers (Smilax spp.). There are several common species of briers including the two-seeded Catbrier or Common Greenbrier (Smilax rotundifolia), Laurel Greenbrier (Smilax laurifolia), and the one seeded Bullbrier (Smilax bona-nox). The Bullbriers also have bristly edged leaves, square stems and a large, thick knobby rootstock. The Catbrier has no bristles on its leaves. It has round or angular stems, and a long thin rootstock.

All of the Briers provide a delightful nibble in the form of new growth of stems, leaves and tendrils. They can easily be collected as you hike through the woods. These young shoots may be prepared and eaten like asparagus. Most of the hundreds of Briers I have sampled have a very pleasant slightly sour taste with a crunchy tender texture. The one exception was an arrowhead shaped bullbrier I sampled in northern Florida, which had a disagreeable musky overtone in its flavor. With a little more ambition the roots can be dug to make a refreshing drink, gelatin substitute or jelly from the red dried root powder. Mixing the root starch with water and heating on a fire until hot makes Bullbrier syrup. Add water or more starch to adjust the thickness of the syrup. The Bullbriers are the superior species to use for root starch (Peterson, 1978).

Some of the first wild edibles to appear in the spring are the Spring-beauties (Claytonia spp.), Toothworts (Dentaria spp.), Indian Cucumber-root (Medeola virginiana), and Garlic Mustard (Allaria esculenta). All four of these plants are real spring treats and make great trail nibbles. Only harvest the delicate corms of the rare spring-beauty and Indian Cucumber-root if the plants are abundant. The Toothworts provide a small pungent radish-like root that is fine by itself or in salads. Use the tender young leaves of the toothworts as salad greens or cook as with other greens. The Indian Cucumber-root taste reminds me of cucumbers with a little more crunch.

Toothwort

    Fiddleheads are also spring favorites. Fiddleheads are the tightly curled shoots of ferns including the Bracken (Pteretis aquilinum), and Ostrich (Pteretis pensylvanica). Studies in Japan have suggested that a lifelong consumption of Bracken Fiddlehead ferns may contribute to stomach cancer, but other studies suggest Ostrich Fern pose no such danger. Fiddleheads are best sautéed. Boil fiddleheads before sautéing to remove excess tannin.

Ostrich Fern

Spring Violets (Viola spp.) are not only beautiful but highly nutritious as well. Prepare young leaves as a potherb, use in salads, or make into a nutritious tea. According to Euell Gibbons one half cup of the leaves contains as much vitamin-C as four oranges and exceeds the U.S.D.A. daily allowance for vitamin-A. The flowers are also said to be three times richer in vitamin-C than oranges. Do not eat yellow flowered species or the unrelated and poisonous African Violets.

Violets

Wood Nettles (Laportea canadensis), Stinging Nettle (Utrica dioica) and Slender Nettle (Utrica gracilis) are frequent residents in and around wet hardwood forests. Use caution when collecting these stinging plants. If they do not contain stingers then you have probably found Clearweed (Pilea pumila) or False-nettle (Boehmaria cylindrica), both members of the Nettle family.

Solomon's-Seal (Polygonatum spp.) shoots can be prepared as asparagus. Their roots are also a delicious treat that must be harvested in moderation, as this plant is rare in most areas. Additionally each seal on the root represents one year of growth, so it can be easily determined how many years an old plant has struggled to survive. Harvesting the shoots will not destroy the plant, but taking the root will. False Solomon-Seal looks very much like Solomon-Seal except has the berries growing only on the termini whereas the "True" Solomon-Seal the berries grow along the entire length of the stem at the leaf joints. The roots of False Solomon-Seal (Smilacina racemosa) have "seals" but are smaller and yellowish and are not edible. The young shoots of False Solomon-Seal can be prepared like asparagus. The extremely poisonous Mayapple (Podophyllum peltatum) roots look similar but do not contain "seals."

Wild Ginger (Asarum canadense) is also in season and can be used just like the unrelated commercial variety.

Wild Ginger

Cleavers or Goosegrass (Galium aparine) is one of my son's favorite wild edibles because it will cleave to your clothes when you pick it. Cleavers can be prepared as a potherb or in salad. A coffee substitute can be made from the dried crushed seeds of this relative of the coffee plant.

Goosegrass "cleaving" to my son's shirt

Goosegrass

The Redbud Tree (Cercis canadensis) can be seen from a great distance when its pink or lavender flowers come into bloom. There are very few trees that can rival its beauty in bloom. These delicate flowers can be added to salads. The small pods can be sautéed or boiled.

Redbud

The Black Locust (Robina pseudo-acacia) flowers make great fritters. Black Locust seeds, roots, and leaves are all poisonous. The pulp of the unripe pods of the thorny Honey Locust (Gleditsia triacanthos) is a honey sweet nibble, however their seeds and skin are poisonous. Do not mistake the Kentucky Coffee Tree (Gymnocladus dioica) with the Honey Locust. The pulp and raw seeds from the Kentucky Coffee Tree are poisonous.

Spring Cress (Cardamine bulbosa) makes a great salad or potted herb. Grind the roots and leaves to make a horseradish substitute. Ramps or Wild Leeks (Allium tricoccum) are another great spring wild edible. They have stood the test of time as a favorite spring wild edible. This member of the Lily family has the unmistakable odor of onion as do all members of the nonpoisonous onion group. Other poisonous look–alikes such as Death Camas, Crested Dwarf Iris, Blue Flag, Yellow Flag, and other Irises do not have the onion odor.

The undisputed champion of spring wild edibles is the Morel (Morchella spp.). More spring foragers seek this delicacy than any other. Its superior flavor has also made it the champ among mushroom hunters as well. Look for morels primarily in March through May. Ensure positive identification of this delicacy in a good mushroom identification guide. Become familiar with their poison look-alikes, the false morels.

Wild Morel

Morels ready to go into the dehydrator

Morels in gravy

Devil's Walking Stick

My first introduction to Devil's Walking Stick (Aralia spinosa) was as boy in the hill country of southern Indiana. I spent most of my free time romping through the woods on various adventures. Occasionally while tearing through a thicket leading down a steep hill I would lose my footing in the forest debris. Inevitably I would reach out to grab a sapling to stop my descent. I would often find my hand clutching a disagreeable handful of Devil's Walking Stick thorns. The thick stout thorns of this shrubby tree would leave my hands stinging and bleeding. After a couple similar encounters I began to pay more attention to this otherwise innocuous plant. Like the Stinging and Wood Nettles I began to remember where stands of these plants grew and passed with caution whenever in their domain. These plants had me so well trained, I even began to recognize potential habitats in areas in which I was not familiar. Although I grew to have much respect for the members of the plant kingdom that inflicted pain, there was no love lost between us. This all changed as my education in the world wild edible and medicinal plants began to increase. As I had discovered with Nettles, Devil's Walking Stick had virtues other than it's stinging repartee.

Devil's Walking Stick is known by many names including Hercules Club and Angelica Tree. The first two names were apparently derived from its thorns and the dermatitis reaction it may inflict in certain individuals. This reaction is similar to poison ivy and results from skin contact with the bark and other parts of the plant. I am not allergic to Poison Ivy and I have never personally contracted dermatitis from Devil's Walking Stick. I have noticed an increased level of irritation and redness resulting from a Devil's Walking Stick thorn prick when compared to similar punctures from other thorny plants.

The Angelic Tree reference probably comes from its similarity to the unrelated Angelic Plant (Angelic atropurpurea) or from its own particular beauty. Devil's Walking Stick is a shrubby tree that often grows in clusters between six and thirty feet tall. It has large doubly compound leaves and the entire plant including the leaves grows thorns. The leaflets are oval, toothed and pointed. In late summer it grows very large clusters of small tiny white flowers that highlight the tree's beauty. Tiny black berries follow the flowers and similarly adorn the tree with beauty. This native plant is found throughout eastern North America, Asia, and other places in North America where it has been introduced.

Devil's Walking Stick is a member of the Ginseng family as are other members of the Aralia genus including Spikenard (Aralia racemosa), Wild Sarsaparilla (Aralia nudicaulis), and Bristly Sarsaparilla (Aralia hispida). The roots of these three members of the genus Aralia are used to make an aromatic tea. However, Devils's Walking Stick roots are probably poisonous and should be judiciously avoided. The berries are also poisonous and guinea pigs have reportedly died of eating the seeds (Brill, 1994).

The new shoots and young leaves of Devil's Walking Stick are edible, plentiful, easy to collect, and delicious. In early spring, around April in southern Indiana, the new year's growth emerges from the woody stalk. The top most or apical bud produces the crown jewel of the edible part of this plant. Bend the tree stalk down with a gloved hand or other protective means and snap the entire green new growth from the top. Anything longer that has developed spines may be too far developed for eating. Remove the tough outer basal leaves and boil the remaining stalk and young tender leaves. The resulting vegetable has a texture similar to asparagus and a taste unique unto itself. I tried to categorize the flavor to similar domestic vegetables, but it really does not taste like anything else. I just tell people that it tastes like Devil's Walking Stick and it is very good. Devil's Walking Stick can regenerate the apical bud growth. I have not yet tested how often you can harvest from an individual tree, but it appears that once a season will do little damage. A friend of mine with a Korean wife reported that when his wife first encountered these familiar plants in the U.S., she excitedly collected them on several occasions and served them with the family dinner. The book titled *Cornucopia* reports these delicacies should be chopped, boiled and served with rice and vinegar (Facciola, 1990). Other uses of this decorative tree are as an ornamental plant and for making walking sticks with some or all of the defensive thorns removed.

Devil's Walking Stick

Devil's Walking Stick in Bloom

Summer

The summer is primarily notable for the various Brambles (Rubus spp.) that are available just about anywhere the light can penetrate the forest. These include Blackberries, Raspberries, Dewberries and others (see the Big Tenth).

Sulphur Shelf (Polyporus sulphurus) or Chicken-of-the-Woods can be found in late summer and fall. This is a conspicuous yellow or orange shelf mushroom that grows on trees, preferably oaks. The tender outer edges can be eaten until they become woody. Sauté or boil Sulphur Shelf mushrooms before freezing to preserve and prevent the hardening process.

Fall-Winter

In the fall, massive quantities of acorns from Oak Trees (Quercus spp.) and other Nuts become easily attainable. Leach the acorns of their tannin by boiling in several changes of hot water. Continue until the water no longer stains. Make sure you do not pour any cold or warm water on them as this will fix the tannin. The acorns of the white oaks contain less tannin than those from the red or black oaks, and as such are easier to prepare.

There are many other nuts free for the picking, including Hickory (Carya spp.), Black Walnut (Juglans nigra), Butternut (Juglans cinera), Beech (Fagas grandifolia), and Pecan (Carya illinoensis). Most of these nuts taste better when dried for a few weeks, particularly the Black Walnut and the Butternut.

Pawpaw

Mid to late September in southern Maryland is Pawpaw season. As I brush through the leaves of the large Pawpaw patch found on my wooded lot, the unmistakable odor of the Pawpaw leaves permeates the air. The very nature of this smell defined the tree for the Cherokee Indians. They called it Disugi, which means it stinks (CF, Vol XV, No 6). To assure you that these large oblong leaves are Pawpaw and not the similarly shaped leaves of other large-leaved trees like hickories or the Umbrella Tree of the Magnolia family, bruise the leaf and take a whiff. If the tree is a Pawpaw you will smell the unforgettable odor of Disugi. The flower also possesses the same offensive odor. The Hickories, Buckeyes and Horse Chestnut leaves have compound leaves with fine teeth. The Pawpaw has an untoothed simple leaf like the Magnolias. The Magnolias are evergreen and the leaves are relatively odorless when bruised.

The Pawpaw is the only member of the Annonaceae or Custard-Apple Family in North America. There are two members within this family, Pawpaw (Asimina triloba) and Dwarf Pawpaw (Asimina parviflora). The Pawpaw is known mostly as a southern tree, but can be found as far north as Michigan and southern Ontario and as far west as Texas and southern Iowa. The Dwarf Pawpaw can be found in pine lands or oak woods from Florida to Mississippi to southeastern Virginia (Fernald, 1950).

The Pawpaw has a rich history of folklore surrounding it. It goes by several names including, Hoosier Banana, Michigan Banana, Fetid Shrub, Custard Apple and many others. James Whitcomb Riley, a prominent poet from southern Indiana, said that eating a Pawpaw was like eating a custard pie without the crust. There have been songs and poetry written about Pawpaws, including one traditional southern song, "Way Down Yonder in the Pawpaw Patch."

The Pawpaw is North America's largest native fruit growing from 1.5 to 4 inches long. As the green kidney shaped fruits ripen they develop brown or black blotches, much like a banana. The fruit is relatively pest resistant until it ripens and falls to the ground. When they lay on the ground the fruits fall prey to many insects, primarily ants and a multitude of animals. Once you have experienced the other smell associated with Pawpaws, the intoxicating fragrance of the ripe fruit, you will understand all the hoopla. The smell and taste of the Pawpaw is somewhere between a banana and a pear with texture similar to an overripe banana. As you bend down to pick the ripe Pawpaws from the ground you will begin to smell your way to the hidden treasures camouflaging themselves amongst the leaves.

The fun of finding and collecting the Pawpaws is only exceeded by the fun of eating them. If you pick them off the ground, they are probably ripe, and you can eat them as they are. Do not eat the seeds or the very bitter skins. You will find it nearly impossible to eat a Pawpaw without sucking the custard like pulp off the many large brown seeds found throughout. Just tear the Pawpaw in half, squeeze the contents into your mouth, and spit the seeds out much as you would watermelon.

If the Pawpaws are hard and not pliable when squeezed, they may be further ripened on your windowsill. According to Euell Gibbons, this fruit should not be allowed to ripen in your house as the fragrance will become overwhelming and turn your family against them. I have found this to be no more of a problem than allowing bananas to ripen in the house.

The other way you can enjoy Pawpaws is by using them in recipes for pies, cookies, breads, cakes and puddings. To use them in recipes they must first be pulped. To do this, again tear the pawpaws in half and squeeze the contents into a ricer or other sieve. Avoid allowing bits of skin to fall into the seed pulp mixture. Press the mixture through the sieve and the resultant watery pulp is now ready to be used in recipes. If substituting in recipes for bananas, remember that the Pawpaw pulp is significantly more watery than banana pulp. Here are a couple of recipes I use for Pawpaw pulp:

Pawpaw Pie

1 c. Pawpaw Pulp
1 3/4 c. milk
Instant vanilla pudding mix (6 cup yield)
1 banana
1 pie crust
Whipped topping

Directions: Prepare and bake your favorite pie crust. Prepare instant pudding, substituting 1-cup pawpaw pulp for 1 cup of milk, as directed by directions on box for pie filling. Pour pie filling into cooled baked crust. Slice banana and evenly place slices on top of pie filling. Spread whipped topping over top of bananas and pie filling. Chill in freezer one hour before serving.

Pawpaw Bread

1 cup pawpaw pulp
1/2 cup sugar
1/2 cup plain nonfat yogurt
1/4 cup margarine, melted
1 teaspoon vanilla extract
2 eggs
2 cups all-purpose flour
1 teaspoon baking powder
1/2 teaspoon baking soda
1/4 teaspoon salt
1/2 cup chopped pecans, toasted
Baking spray with flour

Directions: Whisk first 7 ingredients in a large bowl until well blended. Add flour and next 3 ingredients. Add pecans. Spoon batter into an 8-1/2 x 4-1/2 x 3-inch bread pan coated with baking spray and flour. Bake at 350 degrees for 1 hour or until an inserted toothpick comes out clean. Cool for 10 minutes. Remove from pan and cool completely before serving.

Most Pawpaws are highly perishable and delicate, and as such, are not currently good candidates for commercial cultivation. However, if you consider that the wild apple is a crabapple-sized fruit that has been developed into over 8000 cultivars, you can appreciate the commercial potential of this wonderful fruit. Pawpaw's attributes of flavor, color, texture and seed count varies greatly from tree to tree. There is currently an effort underway to select for commercially viable cultivars based on superior attributes.

Pawpaw pie surrounded by pawpaws

Pawpaw Cultivation

Pawpaws prefer soil of ph from 5 to 7. Saplings do better in shade but larger trees will benefit from full sunlight. Trees will also tolerate shade as they are usually found as an understory tree in nature. Pawpaws are true to seed and need to be stratified below forty degrees for ninety to one hundred and twenty days. The brittle one foot long taproot is first to grow and as such makes it difficult to transplant successfully. For more information about Pawpaws contact the Pawpaw Foundation at:

The Pawpaw Foundation
P.O. Box 23467
Washington, DC 20026

Pawpaw Tree

Persimmons

The American Persimmon Tree (Diospyros virginiana) is the only North American member of the Ebony Family. They also produce North America's largest berry, the Persimmon. The orange fruit of the American Persimmon is 3/4 to 1 inch in diameter and is often mottled with brown or black patches when ripe. The name Diospyros is of Greek origin and roughly translates to food of the gods (Pyros means food or grain and Dios means God or Zeus). There are a couple of lesser-known variations of American Persimmon, the Texas Persimmon (Diospyros texana) and the Hairy Persimmon (Diospyros virginiana var pubescens). Persimmons can be found in most of the eastern United States, from Kansas to Connecticut in the north and from Texas to Florida in the south. Once you get familiar with the blocky looking bark and the slender lance shaped leaves of this tree, it will become easily recognizable from afar.

The wood of this tree was once highly prized for making golf woods, but the demand is now low due to composites and metal alloys. A tea can be made from the leaves of Persimmon that is high in Vitamin C.

There are two types of Persimmons worldwide, the American and the Asian varieties. The Asian or Khaki persimmons compose about 160 species and can often be found for sale at your local grocer. Although they are related to the American Persimmon their taste, texture and nutritional values are very different. The larger Khaki Persimmons have the texture of a firm tomato whereas the American Persimmon is dense and gooey. The Khakis have a mild flavor and the American Persimmons are strong. As far as nutritional content is concerned, the following table derived from USDA composition of foods AGRICULTURE HANDBOOK NO. 8 will give you a good idea:

	Khaki Persimmon	American Persimmon	Unit of Measurement
Calories	70	127	/100g
Protein	.58	.80	g/100g
Fat	.19	.40	g/100g
Water	80.32	64.40	%
Iron	.15	2.5	mg/100gm
Vitamin C	7.5	66	mg/100gm

The delicious fruit of the American Persimmon can be found in hardwood forests in the fall and winter after the first frost. I have picked up delicious persimmons as late as February in Indiana. Some folks say that it is important to wait until after the first frost, as the persimmons contain a high tannic acid content that will pucker your mouth. I have found that some trees produce edible fruits much earlier as well. The Persimmons begin to fall after the first frost. They are a delicious sweet treat and are enjoyed by man and beast alike. Deer and opossums have a particular fondness for them. You may catch an occasional opossum sleeping in a Persimmon Tree in which they had fed the night before.

It is all right to shake the tree to get more Persimmons to fall. Do not shake too hard or you will get some unripe ones as well. Just about any Persimmon that has fallen to the ground naturally or from moderate shaking will be perfect for eating. They are full of brown flat seeds that must be discarded when eating.

When growing up in southern Indiana, our family usually had a cache of Persimmon pulp in the freezer. We were served Persimmon Pudding religiously on Thanksgiving and Christmas using my great–grandmother's recipe. This is still one of my favorite desserts. Persimmon Pudding is also a favorite at fall festivals in southern Indiana as well.

The Persimmons must be pulped before using in a myriad of recipes including cakes, cookies, pies, ice cream or puddings. The easiest way to pulp Persimmons is to use a ricer. Push the pulp through the ricer leaving the skins and seeds behind. The Persimmon pulp freezes well. We use it up to a year later with no noticeable degradation in flavor.

Take the opportunity to scout a nearby hardwood forest for Persimmon Trees this fall. Always seek permission before entering private property. Many homeowners with Persimmon Trees may welcome you. They will be overjoyed that you have volunteered to pick persimmons from their lawn, as they are often considered a nuisance and a mess.

Persimmon Tree loaded with Persimmons

Persimmon Pudding

Great-grandmother Rose Guethe

2 Cups American Persimmon Pulp
1/2 cup melted butter
2 cups granulated white sugar
2 eggs
1 1/2 tsp. baking powder
1/2 tsp. Salt
1 tsp. Ground cinnamon
1/4 tsp. Nutmeg
1/2 tsp. Baking soda
1 cup milk
1 1/2 cup flour

Combine pulp, sugar, butter, and eggs. Add all dry ingredients. Add Milk. Mix well. Grease and flour 9x13 pan. Bake at 300° for 1 hour. Cover in foil while cooling to maintain moister pudding.

My son enjoying Persimmon Pudding

Mayapple

Mayapple (Podophyllum peltatum) also known as American Mandrake is a peculiar little plant that grows in great groves on the floor of some wet forests. With their unique umbrella-like leaves they are pretty unmistakable. Every part of the Mayapple plant is extremely toxic and lethal with the exception of the ripe fruit. The fruit becomes yellowish in color and very soft when ripe. Inside the ripe fruit you will find a tropical-like tasting fruit pulp filled with seeds. The seeds must be discarded or spit out if eating the fruit fresh. The taste of Mayapple is pretty unique also, but it reminds me of passion fruit with its lemony tropical flavor. Some of the plants will bear fruit where others may not. If you can find a large collection of the fruit, it may be worthwhile to extract the pulp from the seeds and skin and use the resultant product for jellies, jams, and pies.

The toxicity of this plant cannot be over-stressed, as it is one of the most toxic plants in North American. In the novel *The Light in Forest* by Conrad Richter, the main character, True Son, is a white boy who has been raised by the Indians. The story revolves around True Son's reintegration back to his white family after he has grown up. While they are transporting him back to his white family, True Son collects some Mandrake root so he can use it to kill himself rather than face living with the strange white folks. He never uses the Mandrake and eventually is able to overcome his cultural crises. As a literary tool this was a valid choice, as it has the potential to kill if any poison part of this plant is ingested. It would probably be a horrible death.

On the positive side many of the same constituents that make this plant toxic also make it medicinal. There is still a market for dried, wild Mandrake root for medicinal processing, although it is not nearly as valuable as Ginseng or Goldenseal.

Other uses of this plant also take advantage of its toxic properties. Crushed and boiled Mandrake leaves may be cooled and applied to the skin as a bug repellent or applied to non-edible garden plants. Avoid applying this solution to open sores or cuts.

Mayapple plant in flower

Nodding Wild Onion

Nodding Wild Onion (Allium cernuum) may sometimes be found in wet forests. These are pretty unique plants in two ways. Their peculiar nodding flower stalk will be the first confirming characteristic of this unique member of the onion family. The second is the familiar onion odor of the bruised leaves or bulb. The onion odor will confirm that it is indeed a member of the edible onion family and not any of the poison onion look-alikes. Like all wild onions and garlics, these are great in stir-fry, stews or raw, if not too strong in flavor.

Nodding Wild Onion

Chapter 5: Disturbed Areas

We need the tonic of wildness-to wade sometimes in marshes where the bittern and the meadow-hen lurk, and hear the booming of the snipe; to smell the whispering sedge where only some wilder and more solitary fowl builds her nest, and the mink crawls with its belly close to the ground.

Henry David Thoreau

What is a disturbed area? Often the botanical guides use the terms *disturbed areas* or *waste areas* to describe habitats for various plants. These areas develop most often as a result of man's intervention. For example, a disturbed area is any area where a bulldozer has altered the terrain such as around any building or road. Also any area where heavy cutting of trees or vegetation has occurred will qualify as a disturbed area. Old abandoned farmsteads that have been allowed to go back to nature are probably my favorite disturbed areas. They often encouraged and sometimes nurtured wild edible and medicinal plants as a supplement to their gardens. Disturbed areas are both a unique and distinct habitat for many plants. Some plants thrive in the early and transitional succession environment where they do not have to compete with climax species. Often these environments are also maintained in this static transitional state by mowing, walking, grazing or other activities that preclude climax species competition.

In my capacity as a volunteer naturalist at Maryland's Patuxent Research Refuge, I conduct wild edible plant walks throughout the year. After the initial lecture, I always start my walk right around the visitor control station and parking lot. This is a classical disturbed area. I know I'll be able to easily locate and identify many edible and medicinal plants that will not be readily available once we leave the developed area. This also gives the program participants an opportunity to see a wide variety of edible and medicinal plants they are likely to see in their own backyards or neighborhoods.

Plants that are likely to be found in disturbed areas include many of the common so-called lawn pests: Dandelion, Plantain, Clover, Purslane, and Chickweed. I call them great, free groceries.

As the habitat becomes more shaggy and unkempt, like in the abandoned farmstead example, some other plants begin to appear more frequently. These include Poke, Elder, Wild Asparagus, Amaranth, Lamb's-quarters, Mustards, Purslane, Day-lilies, Jerusalem Artichoke, Peppergrass, and Brambles. These are some of the finest wild edibles available.

Poke

Poke or Pokeweed (Phytolacca americana) is one of the best known wild edibles and has rich folklore unlike any other plant. This plant was mentioned predominantly in Euell Gibbons' book, *Stalking the Wild Asparagus*. The plant and the edible dish have often been referred to as Poke Salad or Salat. This reference has often misguided individuals into believing this plant could be ingested raw. During one of my wild edible walks at the Patuxent Research Refuge, I was explaining the preparation of Poke when one of the participants related how she had only eaten Poke Salad raw. She further went on to explain that she always became ill afterwards. This is a real good indicator that you are either eating the wrong thing, preparing it incorrectly or your body is just not compatible. This is true for domestic or wild edible plants. Personally I have found more domestic foods that disagree with me than wild.

Poke should never be eaten raw and must be prepared by boiling the young shoots for thirty minutes in at least two changes of water to remove toxic phytolaccin compounds. Only shoots of six inches or less should be collected. Any red or purple leaves or tissues must be removed before cooking as well as any unfurled leaves. Ensure no root is attached to the shoots, as all other parts of the plant including mature leaves, stalks, berries, seeds and roots are poisonous.

All this special handling may scare you away from using Poke, but it is truly a first class wild edible. Once the shoots have been thoroughly cooked in at least two changes of water, they may be served immediately plain or with cheese or butter. They may also be added to other dishes or further cooked such as baking with bread crumbs and butter crust. Some say they taste similar to asparagus; others claim they have their own unique flavor. Euell Gibbons recounted in his book, *Stalking the Wild Asparagus*, how the country folk in southern Indiana prefer to prepare their Poke Salad by peeling off the outer layers, rolling in corn meal and deep frying. Since I am from southern Indiana, I will try this method as well, but first I will boil in two changes of water to ensure their safety.

Poke plants are frequent residents of abandoned farmsteads and other disturbed areas. They can be easily located by the presence of last years white skeletal remains often visible throughout the winter, spring and following summer. Poke plants have huge roots that will get to over eight inches in diameter. These roots can be dug up, and transplanted into pots where they will produce throughout the winter in your basement producing succulent white shoots. Poke can tolerate repeated shoot cutting with no apparent damage. They will send up new shoots to replace the old. Pokeberries were used to stain Port Wine, as an arthritis cure (not recommended), and as Indian ink. Additionally the flower tops may also be used to make great fritters. Remove most of the stem during or after cooking with scissors.

Pokeweed

Elderberry

Common Elderberry (Sambucus canadensis) frequents the same environs as Poke and can be easily located by its large panicle structures of buds, flowers, and berries. As in Poke, Elder has a rich folklore in southern Indiana as a favorite for making elderberry wine. My own family were big consumers and producers of this wonderful and unique product and for many years produced some of the finest available anywhere in fifty five gallon batches. Not only do elderberries make great wine but also make great jellies, preserves and pies.

Elderberry

Purslane

Purslane (Portulaca oleracea) along with Spring Beauty (Claytonia spp.) is members of the Portulacaceae family. The succulent purslane was imported from Europe as a garden vegetable and has escaped and thrived as a wild edible in North America. Purslane is an indicator plant of fertile soil and is often an unwelcome immigrant into gardens. However, in Europe this plant is still cultivated and sold as a prime vegetable. As with Chickweed and Lamb's-quarters, Purslane may absorb dangerous levels of nitrate from over-fertilization, particularly synthetic fertilizers. Purslane contains oxalic acid, which gives it a tart flavor like wood sorrel. It is also high in iron and is very high in Omega-3 fatty acids making it a great candidate for cholesterol reduction.

Eat Purslane raw or cooked in water for ten minutes. The fat succulent stems make great pickles. The small black seeds can be ground into flour or added whole to bread.

"I learned from my two years' experience that it would cost incredibly little trouble to obtain one's necessary food, even in this latitude; that a man may use as simple a diet as the animals, and yet retain health and strength. I have made a satisfactory dinner, satisfactory on several accounts, simply off a dish of purslane (Portulaca oleracea) which I gathered in my cornfield, boiled and salted."

Henry David Thoreau

Purslane

Day-lilies

Day-lilies (Hemerocallis fulva) were imported from Asia as a food plant and have been used in China for centuries as a food staple (Gail, 1989). They can be seen growing wild along roadsides, abandoned homesteads or cultivated along highways for erosion control. Day-lilies are an extremely popular landscape flower that can be found in lawns from coast to coast. Extreme caution should be observed when collecting Day-lilies to ensure positive identification is obtained, as Narcissus, Irises, Daffodils, and Atamasco-lily are all poison look-alikes.

Day-lily tubers, shoots, buds, flower, and pods are all edible. The roots of Day-lilies are poisonous, as are the roots on Irish potatoes and should be likewise removed. All edible parts may be eaten raw or cooked. I have found the raw buds sometimes irritate the throat with a burning sensation. Also from personal experience I have also found that over indulgence in the shoots may result in diarrhea. Others have reported this effect from the tubers, buds and flowers as well (Gail, 1989). I have only personally experienced this problem from eating raw shoots. The tubers may be cooked similarly to any potato recipe, while the buds may be cooked like green beans. The Day-lily seed bearing pods may be cut and sautéed, seeds and all, for a unique vegetable. The blossoms may be added raw to salads to add a unique flair and color or may be cooked in recipes similar to those used with squash blossoms. A great recipe book dedicated to Day-lilies is *The Delightful Delicious Daylily* by Peter Gail and is available from Goosefoot Acres (see Appendix B).

Day-Lily

Yellow Flag a poisonous member of the iris family

Chickweed

Common Chickweed (Stellaria media) is a common lawn and disturbed area plant. The small white flowers often appear to have ten petals, but actually have five petals that are deeply cleft into two halves. The young tender greens can be eaten raw or boiled for less than five minutes. This plant was once used for livestock feed, particularly chickens, hence the name. This plant has also been suspected of accumulating toxic levels of nitrates as in Purslane and Lamb's–quarters (Duke, 1992). Star Chickweed (Stellaria pubera) and Mouse–ear Chickweed (Stellaria vulgatum) are also edible.

Yucca

Yucca (Yucca spp.) is known by various names such as Spanish Bayonet (Yucca aloifolia) and Bear Grass (Yucca filamentosa). The primary edible parts of this plant of many uses are the flower petals and buds, which may be eaten out of hand or added to salads. The fruit pulp of the Yucca species with juicy fruit like Spanish Bayonet may also be eaten. Other parts of the Yucca are not edible including the pulp, fruit skin, leaves, and roots. Some sources recommend eating the seeds after grinding, drying and cooking (Elias, 1982). The roots and leaves are filled with poisonous sapponins. The Yucca or Yuca purchased in the grocery store is not related to the Yucca genus. It is a misnomer for cassava root which is a member of the Spurge family (Brill, 1994).

Burdock

Burdock (Arctium spp.) is a biennial like carrot. Like carrot, it also grows a large taproot that can be eaten from the first year growth of the plant. Personally I think the cooked root tastes somewhere between carrot and celery, but better than either. In Japan they cultivate a large variety of Burdock called Gobo, which can be found in most supermarkets. I have found Burdock root for sale in some health food stores in the United States. The boiled leaf stems of the large plant also provide a delectable vegetable, but remove their bitter skins before cooking. The large bloom stalk is the third food provided by Burdock. These must be collected in the spring before the buds appear or the leaves unfurl. Remove all the outer green skin layers, slice and cook like potatoes (Gibbons, 1971).

There are a couple of other plants that look similar to Burdock including Dock (Rumex spp.) and Cockleburs (Xanthium spp.). Dock plants, particularly Red Dock, have very similar looking leaves. The main difference between the leaves of Burdock and Dock are that Burdock leaves are woolly underneath and Dock leaves are not. Red Dock also has red veins in its leaves. All young Dock leaves are also edible. They may require two or more changes of water and the addition of baking soda to reduce bitterness. Cockleburs have similar looking leaves, which are shorter and more stout. They also have similar looking flowers, but remain green whereas Burdock has purple flowers.

Amaranth

Amaranth (Amaranthus spp.) has the same pre-Incan origins as Lamb's-quarter's South American cousin Quinoa. This was the other major grain crop of the Incas. Like Quinoa it never really took off as a major grain source in early European cultures as have many of the other Native American foods. In the United States, Amaranth can be found in about every health food store, as it is a superfood (see Nutrition Enhancers). The small numerous black seeds were the basis of a major grain crop of the Incas. These can be used to make super–nutritious flours. Amaranth flour and its by-products are commonly found in health food stores. The tender young leaves are the other main superfood crop of this wonderful plant. These can be eaten raw or cooked like greens. Many cultivars of this plant species are available from garden seed sources (see Appendix B).

Chapter 6: Culinary Substitutes

All food is the gift of the gods and has something of the miraculous, the egg no less than the truffle.

Sybille Bedford

It is great harvesting wild foods and living off nature's bounty, but often the resulting meal is bland. The good news is that the Earth Mother's pantry comes complete with a great variety of exciting culinary enhancements to spice up your meal. Many of these are very similar to those with which we have grown familiar but some are not.

Salt and Pepper

Salt, pepper, and sugar are the most sought after basics for culinary enhancement. Salt substitutes can be found from many sources, including hardwood ash. That's right, take dry white hardwood ash from your campfire and sprinkle it on your food. It contains a significant amount of edible salt. Wood ash may also be used as a meat tenderizer (Duke, 1992). A common source of salt from the plant world comes from the ashes of Shepherd's Purse (Capsella bursa-pastoris). Burn the plant in a dry pan or on a rock until it becomes totally dry and turns to ash. Shepherd's Purse is also edible as a spring green. Purslane (Portulaca oleracea) is another plant source of salt and can be processed in the same manner. Although it is not really very salty or peppery, dried and powdered Sassafras (Sassafras albidum) leaves, known as gumbo file' in Louisiana, can be used as a salt and pepper substitute.

There are several pepper substitutes including Peppergrass (Lepidium spp.). The seeds of Peppergrass have a taste more like green hot peppers, but with hotness closer to ground white pepper. The dried or fresh seeds from Mustard Family (Brassica spp.) make an excellent pungent pepper. Evening Primrose (Oenothera biennis) root, Pepper–root also known as Cut-leaved Toothwort (Dentaria laciniata) tubers have a radish-like taste. All are good pepper substitutes.

Peppergrass

Sugar

Sugar substitutes can be found from many sources in nature, including wild beehives. Watching bees' flight paths from feeding fields to their hives will eventually lead you to their hives. Incrementally bait bees with sugar water or honey from the spot where you last saw them on their flight path. Once the bees start to visit your bait stations they will walk you to their hives. Use smoke to drug the bees to lethargy before attempting to take part of their honey. Be sure to leave enough to ensure their continued survival as well.

Tapping trees from the Maple family will yield ample quantities of sap for syrup or honey. Hickories and walnuts may also provide saps suitable for making syrup. Sugar maples provide the highest quality and sweetest syrup or sugar. The best time of year to tap trees for sugarin' is in the late winter or early spring when the night temperatures drop below freezing and the days are warm. This will cause the sap to flow. Snow is often still on the ground during sugarin' season.

Choose large, heavily branched trees and drill holes close to the ground. Two-inch deep holes, 7/16" in diameter for a 1/2" spile is the standard, but adjust measurements as required. Pith out the centers of Smooth or Staghorn Sumac (Rhus spp.) or Common Elderberry (Sambucus canadensis) branches with a hot wire to make natural spiles. Beware of Poison Sumac (Rhus vernix) as it is more caustic than Poison Ivy. Drive the spiles into the drilled holes and hang collecting buckets or other containers from them. The sap may flow for days or weeks according to the weather. Trees growing at more northerly latitudes have the most sap flow. This accounts for the predominance of commercial sugarin' ventures in the northern United States and Canada.

Reduce sap by a ratio of at least forty-to-one to yield in high quality syrup. Boil sap to 219 degrees Fahrenheit for syrup and 236 degrees for sugar. Using the freezing method can also reduce the sap. Freeze five one-gallon jugs of sap. Reduce every five gallons to one and a half gallons by freezing solid in one–gallon containers. Melt one third of the ice and mix together with melted sap. Either discard the ice or keep ice for pure nutritious drinking water. Re–freeze the melted sap. Reduce this one and half gallons to three quarts as before. In the last step reduce the concentrated sap over heat to yield about one pint of syrup (McPherson, 1977). Roots of Briers (Smilax spp.), Reed Grass (Phragmites spp.), and Cattail (Typha spp.) can be boiled down in water to make syrups as well.

Staghorn Sumac

Winged Sumac

Coffee

There are myriads of substitutes for this worldwide favorite herbal beverage, although usually without caffeine. Most coffee substitutes require similar processing methods, which includes slow roasting at 200 degrees and grinding, just like the real thing. The most common substitute for coffee is Chicory root (Cichorium intybus). This beautiful plant with its unique indigo flowers is one of my favorite wild flowers. Once you identify this plant with dandelion shaped leaves you will never forget it. Chicory is still blended with coffee in Louisiana. Do not mistake the similar looking edible Blue Lettuces (Lactucca spp.) for Chicory. Blue lettuce flowers have stems attached whereas Chicory flowers attach directly to the stalks. Several years ago there were national processors of coffee adding chicory to their coffee to make it less bitter.

Roast and grind Dandelion root (Taraxacum offinale) for a coffee substitute. The dried seeds from a plant called Cleavers, Goosegrass, or Bedstraw (Galium spp.), a member of the coffee family, make an excellent coffee substitute. Other substitutes include White Oak acorn hulls and seeds of the Kentucky Coffee Tree (Gymnoclaudus dioica). Use only the roasted seeds of Kentucky Coffee as the raw seeds and surrounding pulp are poisonous. Beware of mistaking these seeds for the longer ones found on the poisonous Honey Locust (Gleditsia trianthos). There are many other coffee substitutes, but these are some of the more common ones.

Teas

A complete list of tea substitutes available from nature is too great to cover here, but a sampling of easily obtainable and very delicious ones follow:

Mints - Quiet variant from spearmint to chocolate mint
Pine needles - A surprising mild and mellow high vitamin C brew.
Sassafras roots - One of my favorites with a strong root beer taste and aroma.
Spicebush twigs - Very spicy in a Christmassy sort of way. Great mixed with sassafras.
Red Clover flowers: Smooth and healthful (see Wilderness Medicine chapter).

Red Clover

Dandelion flowers - Mellow and yellow.
Raspberry and Blackberry leaves - Pleasant and mild. **Chamomile flowers** - Mellow and soothing to the gastrointestinal tract.
New Jersey Tea leaves - One of the first Tea substitutes adopted by the colonies during the British Tea embargo.
Persimmon leaves - Caramelly and smooth.
Sweet Goldenrod - Sweet Anise.

Sweer Goldenrod

Bee Balms leaves - These members of the mint family produce very mellow flowery teas. Oil of bergamot (Bee Balm) is used to flavor Earl Gray Tea.

Wild Bergamot

Lemon Balm - Calms the savage beast within (see Wilderness Medicine chapter).

Garlic

Garlic, the king of culinary spice is readily available in nature. Wild Garlic (Allium canadense) with a triple spathe and Field Garlic (Allium vineale) with a single spathe contain the same active ingredient, allicin. Allicin is responsible for claims of domestic garlic's health benefits. Of the two, Field Garlic is more common and more similar to domestic garlic in odor and flavor.

Field Garlic

Onion

Wild Onions (Allium spp.) are also available in the wild. Be very cautious not to confuse with Death Camas (Zigadenus venenosus) or members of the deadly Iris family. Leaves and bulbs of onion are similar to Camas. Camas has a yellowish flowers and grow on a stock where onions have pink or white umbelle flowers and an unmistakable onion smell. All onions, leeks, and garlic have an oniony smell.

Lemon

Lemon substitutes include Smooth (Rhus glabra) and Staghorn Sumac (Rhus typhina) and Wood Sorrel (Oxalis spp.). Really good pink lemonade can be made from a tea of Smooth or Staghorn Sumac berries. Do not confuse the erect red berries of these sumacs with the white drooping berries of Poison Sumac (Rhus vernix). As the name implies Poison Sumac is poison much like its close relatives Poison Oak and Ivy, only worse.

Carrot

Wild Carrot or Queen Anne's Lace (Daucus carota) is not a related species to domestic carrot. It actually is domestic carrot that has escaped cultivated gardens. Wild Carrot has become quite successful and very widespread. This is a biennial and should be eaten in its' first year of growth just as we do with domestic carrot. The second year carrot will have only an inedible woody carrot smelling root. The carrot family contains some of the most poisonous plants in North America.

Water Hemlock (Cicuta maculata), a deadly look–alike member of the carrot family, is considered by many as the most poisonous plant in North America. One mouthful can kill. Currently there are no known beneficial uses for this plant. Not only is this a lethal plant, but it results in an extremely violent and gruesome death, characterized by severe convulsions and excruciating pain.

Another poison look-alike member of the carrot family is Poison Hemlock (Conium maculatum). Although not as poisonous as Water Hemlock, this naturalized import from Europe was popularized by Plato's account of Socrates' death induced by Poison Hemlock. The ancient Greeks considered this plant to be a humane means of capital punishment. Plato's account of Socrates death suggests that Poison Hemlock gradually paralyzes the body from the feet up, leaving the mind lucid until the end (Elliot, 1995). Other accounts indicate that Poison Hemlock alone would induce a much more gruesome death and that the concoction Socrates drank must have been blended with sedatives or other poisons (Coffey, 1993). Here are some defining characteristics of these three similar <u>adult</u> plants:

	Wild Carrot	**Poison Hemlock**	**Water Hemlock**
Stem	**Hairy**	Smooth with Purple spots Hollow Grooved.	Smooth. May or may not have Purple spots Chambered
Leaves	Highly divided	Highly divided. Ill Scented when bruised	**Twice/Thrice compound**
Flowers	Clustered white with **single purple flower** in center. Bracts-stiff, 3 forked	Clustered white	Clustered white
Root	White or Yellow Carrot-like	White Carrot-like	White **branched** Carrot-like or parsnip odor and taste

There is another deadly look-alike called Fool's-Parsley (Aethusa cynapium). It also has smooth skinned stems and ill smelling foliage. There are also other edible carrot look–alikes including anise, dill, and chervil.

Wild Carrot

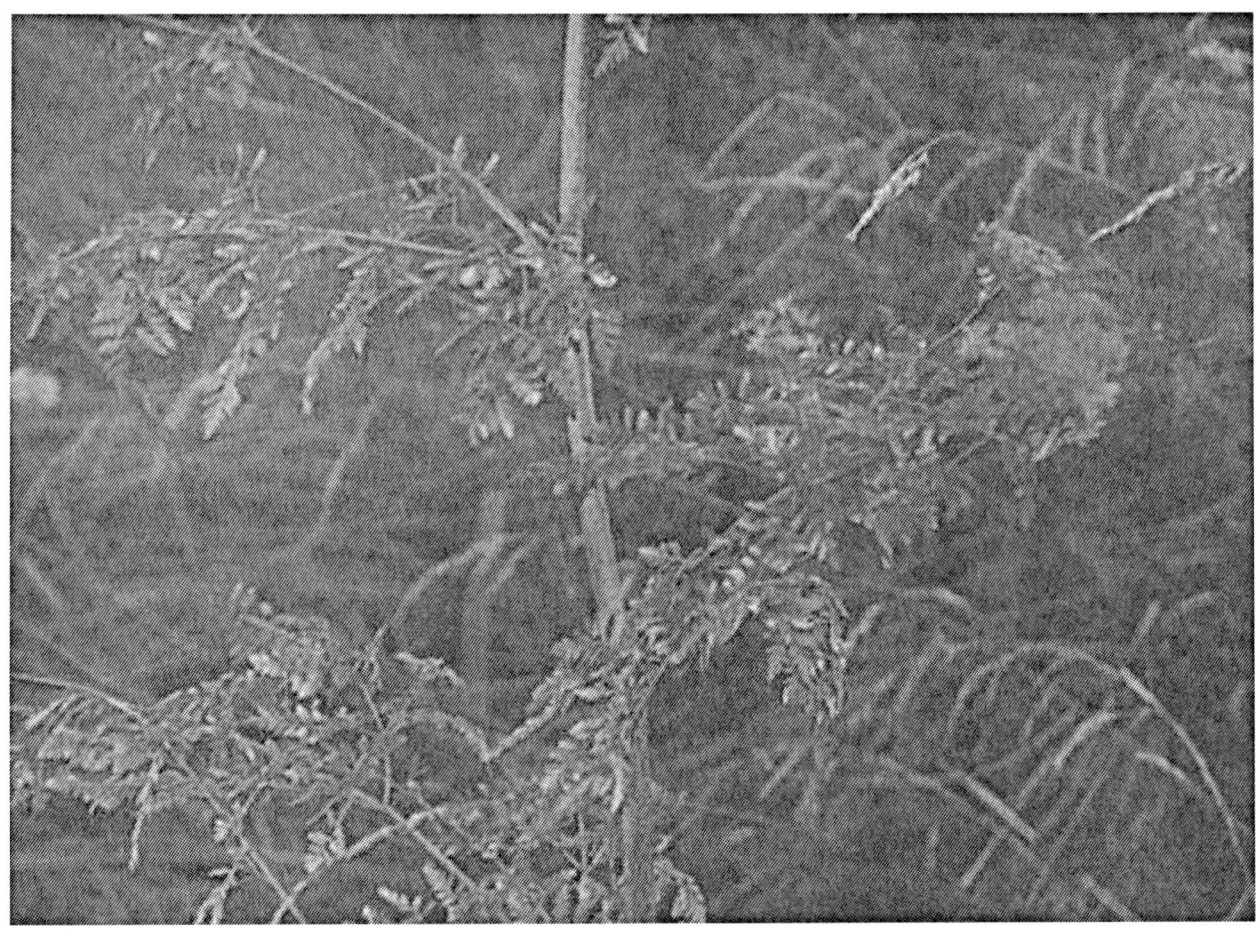

Poison Hemlock

Water Hemlock – The most poisonous vascular plant in North America

Thickeners

Dried and ground Sassafras (gumbo filé) leaves are used as an after-the-fact thickener. Filé is not used during cooking but only at the table according to individual preference. Starch rendered from Greenbriers (Smilax spp.) is used for soup and gravy thickeners. Other flours can be made from Oaks (Quercus spp.), Cattail (Typha spp.) roots starch, and nuts.

Gelatin and Pectin

Gelatin can be made from Greenbrier root starch. Unripe Wild Grapes (Vitis spp.) are also sources of pectin to thicken jellies as well.

Ginger and Cinnamon

A really great ginger substitute is Wild Ginger (Asarum canadense). This beautiful wet woodlands loving plant is not related to domestic ginger, but contains some of the same phytochemicals that give it a ginger aroma and taste. Although it does not exactly have a ginger flavor or smell, Sweetflag (Acorus calamus) root has its own unique sweet spicy aroma and flavor that is similar to ginger. This plant was used to flavor medicines and candies. Sweetflag can be used as a ginger or a cinnamon substitute. Once you smell the wonderful aroma from the bruised leaf or root of this Cattail look-alike you will never forget it.

Horseradish

There are several good horseradish substitutes including Wild Horseradish (Armoracea lapathifolia), Toothworts (Dentaria spp.), Garlic Mustard (Allaria esculenta) roots, Spring Cress (Cardamine bulbosa), roots and seeds from Mustards (Brassica spp.). Horseradish can be made from any of these plants by placing chopped bits of the roots in a blender with your favorite vinegar. Blend until smooth.

Poppy and Sesame Seed

Evening Primrose (Oenothera biennis) seeds make a great substitute for these two seeds on breads and rolls.

Evening Primrose

Parsnips

Evening Primrose (Oenothera biennis) roots make a great substitute for parsnips. Beware of Water Hemlock (Cicuta maculata), the most poisonous plant in North America. This plant has parsnip-like roots that reportedly smell and taste like Parsnips. Less than a teaspoon of this plant can be lethal. This plant bares no resemblance to Evening Primrose, but looks vaguely like Wild Carrot, particularly the flower.

Rennet

Rennet is used to curdle milk in cheese making. Natural plant rennet substitutes can be obtained from strong teas of Yellow Bedstraw (Galium verum), Stinging Nettle (Utrica dioica), or Canada Thistle (Cirsium arvense).

Allspice

Allspice is an all-purpose spice that can be used in main dishes or desserts. Nature has a great substitute for this spice called Spicebush or Wild Allspice (Lindera benzoin). If you have spent any significant time in the woods where Spicebush thrives, you have probably brushed right through it often without even noticing. The fall is the best time to first become acquainted with Spicebush. This is when the plant is in full dress with bright red berries clinging to the length of its limbs. Its fire-engine red pea sized berries will act as beacons to announce its location. Other common red berries that may be mistaken for Spicebush and occupy the same habitat include the Flowering Dogwood (Cornus florida), American Holly (Ilex opaco), and the Ash family (Pyrus spp.). The scratch and sniff test is one way to quickly help you decide if the plant is Spicebush. Scratch the bark of a small twig of the suspect plant and if you get a strong sweet spicy aroma then you probably have found a Spicebush.

Spicebush is a member of the Lauraceae (Laurel) Family that grows up to 12 feet tall. Sassafras is also a member of the Laurel family. Spicebush ranges from southern Michigan and Illinois to SW Maine and southern Ontario, south to North Carolina, Kentucky, Missouri and SE Kansas. The plant also goes by other names such as Feverbush for its fever treating folklore (Fernald, 1950).

As its name implies, Spicebush is a plant from which to make spice. The spice in the Spicebush comes from the fruit. The fresh fruit is not considered edible as is, and some consider it poisonous. However, once the fruits are processed they make an excellent allspice substitute, often considered less harsh and subtler than the original.

To make Wild Allspice, pick a pint or two of fresh berries. Individually squeeze each popcorn-sized seed out of the berry. Most references include the seeds when making Wild Allspice, however at least one reference recommends removal of the seeds first (Brown, 1985). You may want to wear latex gloves for this part of the processing because the berries will stain your fingers. Dry the pitted berries by either using a dehydrator, placing near an open fire, or in your oven set at the lowest temperature. I usually use a dehydrator. Make sure the berries are thoroughly dry before grinding them into powder. If the berries smash rather than grind, they may need to be dried further.

Grind the berries using a mortar and pestle, spice grinder, or coffee grinder. Grind the berries thoroughly and place resultant spice in an old spice jar or other suitable container.

You may use this Wild Allspice anywhere you would normally use Allspice. It is particularly good with venison and beef roasts. You can also use it in cakes, cookies or any other desserts that call for allspice.

Spicebush tea is a wonderful treat you can enjoy year round once you have positively identified Spicebush plants in your area. Make the tea from young leaves, twigs, and bark of the plant. You may want to pick extra leaves in the spring, dry and save for making tea year round. You can also gather the twigs or bark during any part of the year for making tea. Adding milk and honey to this tea will improve the flavor greatly.

Cherokee Indians used all parts of the bush for treating coughs, colds, fever, and croup. They also used it for a spring tonic and as a flavoring for opossum and groundhog (Hamel, 1975). Spicebush plants are very shade tolerant and will easily adapt to the lawn.

My daughter making "Wild Allspice"

Chapter 7: Winter Foods

For me, nature is a religion; I sense in the wilderness the spiritual side of the unknown.

Bev Doolittle

If trying to sort out the diversity of the green wall of nature is intimidating to you during the spring, summer, and fall, then the winter may be equally challenging with its lack of green. When I give my wild edible walks during the three green seasons, participants are always amazed at all of the different plants available for food, medicine and utility. They are even more incredulous that there is anything at all available in winter.

Granted the stark winter landscape is not as inviting and generous as it is during the other three seasons, but there are plant products to be had. All the non-hibernating animals that must continue to earn a living from the landscape have taken most of the easy pickings. A lot of animals, like deer, cannot find enough to eat through the winter. This is particularly true when snow prevents their access to the ground, and many of their numbers starve to death. Fortunately, we humans have learned how to collect, preserve and store food to see us through winter. This should be your first strategy to eat from the land year round, as it is the easiest and gives the greatest abundance.

There are four general categories of foods to found in winter, latent fall crops, persistent winter edibles, late winter arrivals, and underground harvestables.

Latent Fall Crops

The first category consists of those crops that are still available in small quantities that are left over from the fall. Some examples of these are Persimmons, Grapes, and other fruits. I have on more than one occasion found perfectly good Persimmons or Grapes as late as February either still attached to plants or recently fallen to the ground. Other fruits such as Apples, Haws, etc., can also be found. Occasionally Walnuts, Hickory nuts, acorns and other nut crops can be found in abundance in the winter. Usually, though, the local wildlife has found and collected most of this bounty.

Persistent Winter Edibles

What I call the persistent winter edibles are those plants that hang around all winter albeit in a less vigorous state such as Henbit, Dandelions, Plantain, Grasses, etc. American Mountain Ash (Sorbus americana) has edible red berries that can be found throughout the winter. The key for identifying this group of edibles is to just look for whatever green is left and identify the edible members among them. For the most part these plants will be in their most unpalatable state and may need to be boiled longer than usual. The addition of baking soda may help to tenderize and quell some of the accompanying bitterness. The inner bark of Cherry Birch (Betula lenta), White Birch (Betula alba) Black or River Birch (Betula nigra), and Yellow Birch (Betula lutea) can be cooked like pasta or dried and ground into flour. Birch twigs may be used to make a tea. The Cherry Birch contains poisonous Methyl Salicylate and should be used only in moderation (Duke, 1992). Several other tea sources available throughout most of the winter include Staghorn and

Smooth Sumac for making Sumac lemonade from the berries. The Spicebush plant is available year round for making Spice Tea from the small twigs, as are the Pines for Pine Needle Tea.

Our good friend the Prickly Pear Cactus (Opuntia spp.) does not go anywhere in the winter either. It just guts it out through the snow and ice all winter long. The leaves will turn darker and thinner, but they will still be there.

Henbit

Late Winter Arrivals

Late winter arrivals or extremely early spring arrivals consist of a few plants. The most representative of these are Early Wintercress (Barbarea verna) and Yellow Rocket or Wintercress (Barbarea vulgaris). These plants should be used in moderation due to studies linking them to kidney malfunctions (Duke, 1992). Others include Dandelion and Plantain.

When the nights fall below freezing and the days are warmer, it is the time of the year to collect saps from trees for making syrup or sweet drinking water. Along with the Maple trees (Acer spp.), members of the Birch (Betula spp.), Walnuts (Juglans spp.), and Hickories (Carya spp.) can all be used for sap collection. The Maple species will yield sap with the highest sugar content.

Underground Edibles

The underground edibles are where the lion's share of winter forage can be found. Many perennial plants use a strategy of storing reserves in underground parts to survive through winter. Land species such as Day-lilies are a great example. They have tubers that are available year round, but in the winter all their reserves are stored there as the above ground parts die back. It is in the winter that storage tubers such as these are larger and more nutritious than any other time of the year.

Jerusalem Artichoke

Jerusalem Artichoke (Helianthus tuberosus) tubers can be dug from fall until early spring. Jerusalem Artichokes are a member of the Sunflower family. These were one of the staple foods of the North American Indians. These plants should be located during the summer and early fall for collecting their large yellow tubers in the winter as the tubers will not be available until the plant dies back in the fall. Their tubers are only available from the late fall through spring. They have a sweet apple-like taste, thus another common name - Earth Apple. They may be boiled or baked like potatoes or substituted for water chestnuts in chinese recipes. Euell Gibbons was a big fan of pickling the tubers. They are also known as Sunchokes and are often available in grocery stores by this name.

Jerusalem Artichoke

Garlic Mustard

Garlic Mustard mentioned in the Big Ninth and the Wet Hardwood Forest section of this book has large fleshy roots with horseradish flavor. If you locate large stands of these mustards when they are green or by their brown dead remains, locating their roots will not be difficult.

Go to the Water

Areas of water such as creeks, rivers, ponds and lakes have much stored food to harvest. The cattails, which usually grow in large stands, are easy to locate in the winter by their downy seed heads. During the winter the roots of these plants are storing all of the reserves for next spring's growth. There are two basic products that can be harvested from cattails in the winter, the root starch and the corms. The root starch is obtained by collecting the roots and breaking them apart under water in a container. The freed root starch will be suspended in the water. Let the starch settle over night and the water can be poured off. The resultant flour is nutritious and said to contain gluten, which is necessary for bread to rise. The flour can be used to make gruel, thicken stews and soups, or used as flour extender. The other product from winter cattails is the corm, which is a shoot that stays under the mud until the spring. These crisp tender delicacies can be eaten raw if you are willing to risk Giardia infestation or when cooked can be eaten safely.

Another harvestable water plant is Arrowhead (Sagittaria spp.) which was a staple food of the North American Indian. It was also a major trade commodity between tribes and with the immigrant European population. This plant was known to the North American Indian as Wapato (Wa pa too) and also by the name Duck Potato. Ensure positive identification as this plant has a poison look-alike, Arrow Arum (see Aquatic Wild Edibles for details). Arrowhead sends out runners from the root base and forms the Duck Potatoes away from the main plant. The main plant actually dies off and the next year's growth comes from the Duck Potatoes. This feature makes this plant a different kind of a perennial. North American Indian squaws would brave the frigid fall and winter waters, dislodging the Wapato from the muck with their toes. The Duck Potatoes would float to the surface where they were collected in baskets.

Another similar food source is the American Lotus (Nelumbo lutea) which provided a copious food source for North American Indians. The American Lotus plant grows large sweet potato-like tubers along a root system that may stretch fifty feet or more. Although harvesting these tubers can present a challenge as well, they are reported to be delicious. Be especially careful when harvesting winter roots to ensure you avoid the deadly roots of the Irises and the Water Hemlock.

The water also offers sustenance from the other side of the food chain as well, in the form of animal life like Frogs, Turtles, Clams and Fish. Many of these can be easily found and captured as discussed in the next chapter.

Chapter 8: Critters

"All courageous animals are carnivorous, and greater courage is to be expected in a people, such as the English, whose food is strong and hearty, than in the half starved commonalty of other countries."

Sir W. Temple

When I was less than twelve years old my appetite for the outdoors was only partially whetted by a few small fields and stands of woods near my house and an occasional visit to my great grandmother's farm in the country. I loved going to my great grandmother's house for she had almost forty acres with other large uninterrupted parcels of woods and fields surrounding her. When I was twelve we moved to the country not far from my great grandmother. This was when my nature odyssey really began. There was a large creek and several ponds not far from my house with lots of fields and woods as well. These all made up my playground and I spent countless hours following my curiosity to wherever it would lead. More often than not I could be found walking down the middle of the creek or wading in ponds looking for the various critters that lived there. I soon found by observing where and how these animals lived, hunted, and hid from danger. I learned how to outwit them and bring them to my table using minimal equipment or effort.

Water Critters

Frogs

I knew all the haunts where the frogs hung out. Frog hunting at night is the traditional method of acquiring them. This is usually accomplished by using a flashlight for blinding them and using a fish spear or frog gig. A net is as good as a gig for catching frogs. Hand hunting at night is difficult because even if you do grab them before they jump, they will usually slip out of your hands because they are covered in a slimy mucous. No matter how you hunt them at night, there is hardly anything more fun than gigging frogs when the gigging is good.

I went frog gigging at night often and became quiet successful, but I was never so successful as I was when I learned how to hunt them during the day. Hunt them during the day, are you crazy? They only come out at night, well not exactly. The largest frog I ever caught was during the day and it weighed in excess of two pounds. This particular frog had found himself a very secure hunting position under a bridge protected by concrete. During the day he would sit all day long with his nose sticking out of the concrete to catch unwary insects. He was shaded all day sitting in moist mud and a little water. If danger came he would just crawl back further into his concrete fortress. Because all of his needs were fulfilled during the day he was able to hunt in the day and as well at night. The way I caught this particular bugger was to dangle a fishing fly from the top of the bridge and like a good frog he ate the fly and I ate him.

This was not the real revelation in daytime frog hunting. That came about a year later when I was checking out one of the ponds in the early morning hours and I spied a large bullfrog hanging out in the daylight. I did not think this was too unusual, because I had seen many bullfrogs out during all hours of the day, just not in the same quantity as at night. As I slowly sneaked up on the frog in a futile attempt at catching him, he didn't jump in the water as they usually do. He did something entirely unexpected and turned around and crawled back into a hole in the embankment. I kept my eyes on the hole and ran over and stuck my hand up inside it. I retrieved him and two others from that hole. I started checking other holes and within a period of about forty-five minutes I had collected sixteen eating size bullfrogs. To be sure there are several inherent dangers in collecting frogs this way. The hole may belong to something other than a frog, like a water moccasin, muskrat, or snapping turtle. Southern Indiana only has water moccasins in one county. At the time the Department of Natural Resources was claiming Indiana had none at all. Ignorance is bliss. We definitely had muskrats and snapping turtles so I avoided holes that were too big for bullfrogs. I never did grab hold of anything but frogs and mud. Let caution be your guide, but I probably wouldn't try this in water moccasin country.

Bullfrogs (Rana catesbeiana) are the largest North American frogs and grow large meaty legs. There are other frogs that get big enough to eat such as the Green Frog (Rana clamitans), Northern Leopard Frog (Rana pipiens), Southern Leopard Frog (Rana sphenocephala). There are others, but ensure they are not an endangered or threatened species before adding them to your menu. There is a species of frog called a Pickerel Frog (Rana palustris) that looks very much like the Leopard frog that is poisonous to eat and will make you very sick. The Pickerel Frog has parallel rows of rectangular dark blotches on its back, while the Leopard frogs have rounded non-parallel rows or a row of dark blotches on their backs. The Pickerel frog occurs generally on the eastern half of the continent where the Leopard frogs range almost all the way from the east to West Coast.

Once you catch your larder of frogs make sure to clean and eat the whole thing. In restaurants and grocery stores they only use the back legs. There is about fifty percent more meat found on the front legs, sides and back that taste identical to the rear legs. Frogs are one of the easiest animals to clean. Cut off the head and all four feet. Pull the skin off like a latex glove. Cut open the stomach and pull out the entrails. Wash thoroughly and you are ready to cook. Frogs are delicious just about any way they are prepared. They are usually prepared by breading and frying. They taste remotely like chicken, but they have a unique flavor that is more delicate in texture and taste. Frogs are truly gourmet fare.

Bullfrog

Snapping Turtles

My first introduction to snapping turtles was while fishing at one of my favorite ponds. For the first time ever I was catching bass on this pond. Usually I just caught sunfish or catfish. That day was different and I had a stringer full. I really hadn't paid much attention to the snapping turtles until that fateful day when they fired the first shot in our war that summer. A good friend of mine was on the other side of the pond and I beckoned him over to check out my stringer full of bass. When he arrived, I proudly showed him my stringer full of bass heads. That is right, bass heads. I do remember that there was one bass that had some of his body left, but it too had bites taken out of it. From that moment on we declared war on the snapping turtles.

Using eight to ten foot long static fishing lines baited with hot dogs launched our first counter offensive. These worked really well and we caught about half a dozen in the first week. Next I built a turtle trap that consisted of a four-foot square frame made of two by fours laying wide side down. Next I drove sixteen-penny nails in about one inch on the inside perimeter. This left most of the nail protruding inside the square. Finally I constructed a two-foot deep basket that attached to the bottom of the frame. I tied a length of rope to one side of the baited trap and hauled it out a safe distance from the shore. The bait may not be required, as turtles will sun themselves on anything that floats. The turtles climbed onto the two by four frame of the trap and either from the attraction of the bait or fifty-percent probability will slide across the nails into the basket when it departs. The nails will not allow him to get his shell back up out of the basket. It is a one way trap. Haul the trap in with the line and the turtles are yours. With the addition of this trap we pretty much cleaned the lake out of Snappers and we had some mighty good eating for our trouble.

We would always bring the turtles home alive and throw them into our turtle holding pens, which were whiskey barrels filled with water. Occasionally the turtles would have leaches on them. We found the easiest and safest way to remove the leaches from a snapping turtle was to pour salt on them. In less than a minute the leaches will release their hold and they can be easily shaken out. We would generally feed the turtles clean food for a few weeks to clean out their systems before we would eat them.

Cajun's in Louisiana use the method described above for catching frogs to catch turtles. They feel for the non-business end of the turtle and pull them out by their tail and hind legs. I think I will reserve that method for frogs only. The traps and line work great for turtles.

Whenever you are dealing with snapping turtles, respect is in order. Their jaws are easily capable of removing flesh or fingers. They are quite eager to demonstrate their prowess in this area. To clean a turtle first remove the head with a hatchet or ax. Be careful both the turtle's head and the ax are dangerous. Once the turtle's head has been removed it can and will bite for about an hour. It just cannot strike as it could when it was attached to the body. The body of the turtle will also continue moving up until you put the skinned a de-shelled parts into the cooking pot. It is widely held that there are thirteen different types of meat in a turtle as there are two types on a chicken, white and dark. I never really bothered to verify that there are thirteen, but there are several different looking meats throughout the turtle. They are all equally delicious. Typically turtle is either fried or made into soup. There are many great turtle soup recipes available in many cookbooks.

The snapping turtle (Chelydra serpentina) grows to a shell length of up to 20 inches and can be found throughout the eastern two thirds of the United States. The Alligator Snapping Turtle (Macroclemys temmincki) grows to a shell length of 26 inches and can be found in the southeastern United States and Illinois and Indiana in the northern range. There are other edible water turtle species, but most are not worth the effort when you try to get any significant amount of meat from them. Land tortoises may contain levels of toxins that are harmful or poisonous to humans. These little guys definitely would not be worth the effort in any event.

Snapping Turtle

Catfish

Much like the incident I described with watching the frog retreat back into its hole I observed catfish retreating under large rocks into embankment holes, and under water tree roots. I soon knew of a couple of secret spots in the creek where I could go fishing with my bare hands and catch fish every time. These catfish, mostly bullheads, in the clear creek water remained hidden during the day and active at night much like the frogs. They too became easy pickings once their hiding places were discovered.

Crayfish

Crawdads or Crawdaddies as we preferred to call them were one of our favorite critters to hunt in the creeks. We would use our bare hands and sometimes our bare feet to catch these little delicacies by the hundreds every summer. The ones we caught in the local southern Indiana creeks were smaller than those raised on farms in Louisiana and Texas today, but tasted just as good, probably better, because we caught them ourselves. We were able to find a species of crayfish that was larger than most of the commercial varieties at the bottom of lakes. We accomplished this by snorkeling down to about six to ten feet. This was sort of like Florida lobster hunting, only the lobsters were smaller and the water colder and darker.

Using a baited conical minnow trap left on the creek bottom for a couple of days would always catch quite a few crawdads. The only other way I discovered for catching them in large quantities at once was to find their breeding groups in the spring where hundreds congregated together. We could never really put a dent on their vast numbers, but when we found these larger concentrations we caught more quickly.

Prepare crayfish as you would lobsters or shrimp. They can be boiled in salted water or crab boil. The tail meat can also be liberated from the tail, breaded in flour, cornmeal, or cracker crumbs and sautéed. Any recipe calling for shrimp or lobster will suffice. Do not forget about all of those great Cajun Mudbug recipes either.

Crayfish ready to eat

Clams

Freshwater clams were also always easy to locate once we discovered the silty and sandy creek bottoms they preferred. These were really easy to collect. The only problem we had was we could never cook them long enough to make them tender. They tasted very good but were as tough as tire rubber. I have not collected any in a long time, but the next time I get freshwater clams, I'll put them in the crock pot all day and grind them up as with stuffed clam recipe. This should even make tire rubber soft. Before collecting freshwater clams ensure they are not endangered or protected with your state Department of Natural Resources.

Land Critters

Crayfish

When I was a small boy I thought the crayfish that lived on the land and made the crayfish mounds were just bigger versions of those who lived in the water. I learned much later that these land loving crayfish that make their mounds in low-lying fields are vegetarians unlike their water loving cousins. They excavate down into the ground to the water level pushing the mud up to form their mound. The mud they excavate out becomes their mound. Looking down through the opening of these mounds during the day, the crayfish can often be seen in a defensive position waiting for nightfall.

At night they come out of their mounds in force where they feast on vegetation. In large numbers they can become very destructive to crops. If you see a field filled with crayfish mounds, secure permission from the landowner to help rid him of these crop pests. They are very easy to catch at night with a flashlight. Their eyes will glow when the light strikes them. Grab them on the thorax behind the pinchers and toss them into your booty bag. They are prepared just like their water loving cousins (Gibbons, 1962).

Possums

Opossum or possum was one of the staple foods of the Clampetts in the Beverly Hillbillies. Possum and cornbread was also a meal my grandfather was always saying he missed from his childhood. Well you know what they say, "Be careful what you wish for, you might get it." This was the case with my grandfather, because one summer I was bound and determined I was going to make his wish come true, which I did with great success.

Possums are primarily nocturnal animals. They are not very smart, they do not move very fast, and they are not very ferocious. Despite all this they have been on this earth for more than 75 million years. They have accomplished this primarily by having large litters of young. They can be easily located with a flashlight or the headlights of your car where they spend a large amount of their time dining on road kill. Besides road kill, they really like persimmons and can often be found hanging upside down from persimmon tree limbs during the day sleeping. I guess they forget sometimes that they are supposed to hide before daybreak. Possums are opportunist and will eat just about anything dead or alive that is too slow to get away from them. I recall one morning looking at a dead cow carcass and seeing both a possum and another opportunists, a raccoon, crawling out the back end of the dead animal. This lack of pickiness in their diet is also partially responsible for their success as a species.

To catch a possum without a gun requires little skill or stealth. Once you have spotted one, run it down and either kick it or hit it with a stick. Neither of these efforts requires much force, as the object is not to hurt it, but rather to get it to play possum, which they generally will do with the slightest provocation. If they do not play possum with the first blow, strike again. The reason you want to catch possums relatively unharmed is so that you can purge their system for a few days of their gourmet diet of road kill and other delicacies. During this period you can feed them about any fruit or vegetables available.

Cleaning possums is relatively straightforward. Make sure the scent glands are removed from under the legs. They store their fat external to their musculature in greasy globules that can be easily scraped off. If you catch a possum in the fall the fat build up will be substantial. I recommend spring and summer possum for that reason. It is best to parboil possum in water with a little vinegar, bay leaves and onions before baking. Also consider using Spicebush twigs pierced throughout the roast. When baking the possum either wrap with bacon or baste frequently as there is no internal marbling.

Insects

There is much discussion about eating bugs in survival situations, however, bugs should not constitute the majority of your protein consumption as they are usually difficult to obtain in sufficient quantities to fulfill your protein requirements. However, occasionally you may find the mother lode of some edible insects like crickets, grasshoppers or grubs. You may also find only a few as well. The best way to take advantage of these little protein pills is to toss them into soups or stews where their entire nutritional value can be obtained. Grasshoppers and crickets must be stripped of their tough wings and legs before cooking. Grubs can be used as they come from nature. I once made some sautéed crickets for my seven-year-old son and myself. I parboiled them first, and then sautéed in olive oil and garlic. My son thought they tasted like mashed potatoes. I thought they tasted like grasshoppers sautéed with garlic. Their tough skins had to be spit out as they were tough as plastic. There is significant research underway to harness the vast nutritional potential of insects using micro-farming to feed the undernourished population of the world (See Appendix A for the Food Insects Newsletter).

Chapter 9: Wilderness Medicine

"The Lord hath created medicines out of the earth: and he that is wise will not abhor them. Was not the water made sweet with wood, that the virtue thereof might be known?"

Ecclesiasticus 38:4-5

Free herbal remedies from nature are plentiful. Narrowing the scope from the hundreds of medicinal plants listed in the Native American and other medicinal guides can be daunting. There are a few key species however, that have demonstrated their efficacy either in the literature or from scientific studies. This chapter will focus on these key species that can be found locally in many parts of North America. There are many excellent herbal books available on the market today that extensively explore herbal remedies and their efficacy. See the appendix for a list of my favorite herbal books and the bibliography as well for further exploration. Many remedies mentioned in this section are also available in health food stores in various preparations. However, the intent of this treatment is to highlight the popular herbal remedies available directly from nature for common afflictions.

I do not prescribe self-medication and anyone who partakes does so at his or her own risk. There are many inherent dangers with self medication that include, but are not limited to, plant misidentification, misdiagnosis, allergies, synergistic reactions with other medications, lack of rigorous safety studies, and dosage control. If you are in doubt, consult with a competent medical authority before trying any questionable medicinal practice. The information presented here is for educational purposes only and should not be used until you consult your physician. Native Americans and others dependent upon Nature have used medications presented here for their health care.

According to Steven Foster and Dr. James Duke, over forty percent of the United States pharmacopoeia contains at least one component derived from nature (Foster, 1990). Some of these components such as the cardiac glycosides derived from Foxglove (Digitalis spp.) have no synthetic substitute. Others such as salicin from Willow (Salix spp.) have synthetic substitutes, in this case Acetylsalicylic Acid (Aspirin). Nonetheless, many of our modern synthetic medicines originated from Native American and other herbal remedies.

Daily Annoyances

The first medicines from nature's medicine chest are for the same maladies one would look in their own medicine cabinets at home for relief.

Headaches/Aches/Pains/Fever.

The very first natural medicines to become familiar with are the aspirin substitutes. These include the willows (Salix spp.), Cherry Birch (Betula lenta), and Wintergreen (Gaultheria procumbens).

The familiar Black Willow (Salix nigra) can be found just about anywhere there is water in the eastern United States and Canada. Its close relatives, White Willow (Salix alba), Weeping Willow

(Salix babylonica), and Pussy Willow (Salix nigra) also contain the important precursor to aspirin called Salicin. The Salicin can be obtained from the inner bark or small twigs of the tree. The inner bark or small twigs can be either chewed or brewed in a cup of tea. To make tea, add a small bundle, about the length and width of your little finger, to one cup of hot water. The resulting brew will taste medicinal (bitter) much like the taste of aspirin. This remedy is highly effective. As with other aspirin products, large doses may be toxic and even fatal. Use in moderation.

Cherry Birch, the most aromatic of the Birch family, contains the essential oil, methyl salicylate and has a wintergreen flavor. This essential oil is toxic. It may cause harm to the liver and kidneys and may also be absorbed through the skin. Fatalities have been reported (Foster, 1990). The inner bark and small twigs may be used similarly to Willow.

Wintergreen or Tea Berry, as in Tea Berry gum, also contains the essential oil methyl salicylate and should also be considered highly toxic. For my money I'll stick with the willows that are more widespread and safer.

Wintergreen

Cuts/Burns/Abrasions

Burns, sunburns and wounds can be treated with an assortment of medicinal plants including mashed Cattail (Typha spp.) roots, and mashed Burdock (Arctium spp.) roots to make a salve. Cattail leaf ash also makes an excellent antiseptic, antimicrobial and styptic (Meuninck, 1995). Another styptic and antiseptic of some notoriety is mashed Yarrow (Achillea millefolium) leaf.

Yarrow is known by many names including Soldier's Woundwort. A poultice can also be made from a strong tea of Yarrow soaked into a cloth. A strong Stinging Nettle (Utrica dioica) tea applied directly to an open wound is an outstanding hemostat to stop profuse bleeding (Heinerman, 1988). Heal-All (Prunella vulgaris) also known as Self–Heal and Woundwort is beneficial for both internal and external wounds (Moulton, 1977).

Yarrow

Comfrey (Symphytum officinale) contains a compound called allantoin that is responsible for new cell growth. This herb has over a 2000–year history of external use for minor and major wounds. Although there is controversy over its safety for internal use, no such controversy exists concerning its external use. Allantoin is the active ingredient in many over-the-counter skin preparations (Castleman, 1991). Also note that Comfrey was been mistaken for Foxglove and was ingested recently by an elderly couple. This mistake resulted in both their deaths.

Comfrey

Aloe vera has been long recognized as a home remedy for cuts, burns and abrasions. This plant grows wild in much of the southern United States. Another excellent poultice can be made with mashed Plantain (Plantago spp.) leaves applied to the wound and whole leaves applied on top.

Heartburn

If you have a little heartburn after that wilderness stew, brew yourself a little Dandelion (Taraxacum officinale) root tea or a soothing Chamomile (Matricaria chamomilla), Feverfew (Chrysanthemum parthenium) or mint tea. Chamomile and feverfew are closely related members of the compositae family and look similar. Feverfew leaves are cut and dissected where chamomiles are highly dissected and almost lacy. The flower center is conical and the petals bend downward in chamomile. The Cherokee Indians used a Persimmon (Diospyros virginiana) bark tea for heartburn as well (Meuninck, 1990).

Feverfew

Hay Fever

Becca Harber reports that taking 1/2-teaspoon tincture of Purple Coneflower (Echinacea spp.) twice a day for three months before hay fever season and 1/2 teaspoon every half hour during symptoms is an effective treatment for Hay Fever (CF, 1992, J/A).

In his book *Spontaneous Healing,* Dr. Weil recommends taking commercial Stinging Nettle (Utrica dioica) capsules as a superior treatment for hay fever and other allergy symptoms with none of the toxic side effects of antihistamines or steroids (Weil, 1995). The commercial preparations contain one ingredient, dried powdered Stinging Nettle. Stinging Nettle is a high-quality wild edible potherb and tea, and is free for the harvesting. A bottle of the commercially prepared Nettle costs around seven dollars. Boiling or drying and powdering wild Stinging Nettle will easily de-fang the delicate yet effective stinging hairs.

Coneflower

Decongestant

When the Mormons settled into their Promised Land in what is now Utah, they had very little in the way of everyday foodstuffs with which they were familiar. The local Indians introduced to them a piney tasting herb beverage now known as Mormon Tea. Mormon Tea (Ephedra nevadensis) belongs to a very primitive and ancient plant family called Ephedraceae that dates back to the days of the dinosaurs. Another member of this family is Horsetail (Equisetum spp.). The over-the-counter cold medication called pseudoephedrine is a synthetic version of one of the three active ingredients in Ephedra. The other two are ephedrine and norpseudoephedrine. There is also a Chinese species of ephedra called Ma-huang (Ephedra sinica) that contains significantly higher levels of ephedrine where the American Ephedra contains higher levels of norpseudoephedrine.

Although Ma-huang is primarily marketed in health food stores as the natural decongestant of choice, the American version is nonetheless effective as well. The three active ingredients in ephedra are also a powerful stimulant that is stronger than caffeine. Other side effects include an increase in perspiration, heart rate, metabolism and blood pressure. Therefore anyone with high blood pressure should avoid this herb (Castleman, 1991).

Assaults from the Plant Kingdom

As much as I enjoy experiencing the great outdoors, our plant brothers and sisters sometimes like to remind us that this is their home too. I have also observed that the more time you spend in the outdoors, the less frequently this occurs. I think this has something to do with a heightened awareness level, which makes us more sensitive to where we walk and what we step on. Maybe our plant brothers and sisters are just trying to be good teachers by reminded us of this from time to time.

Poison Ivy/Oak/Sumac

Poison Oak (Rhus toxicodendron) and Poison Sumac (Rhus vernix) are not as widely distributed as Poison Ivy (Rhus radicans). Poison Ivy makes up the difference, as it is one of the most diverse and prolific plants in North America, seemingly having no one specific preference for soil type, shade, or moisture content. All three belong to the Sumac family. They exude a milky sap allergen called catechol. Fifty to seventy five percent of the population is allergic to catechol. The allergen can not be transmitted from the blisters of one individual to another but only from the plant, and, once exposed through your own blood. If you are not allergic now, you may easily become allergic upon repeated exposures. Once allergic, you will always be allergic. So far I have been among the lucky and have only shown minor eruptions of two to three bumps only twice in my life. I hope my luck holds out as I am exposed to these plants continuously (Novick, 1994).

The best treatment for these plants is to avoid them. Poison Ivy and Poison Oak both have three leaves. The Poison Oak has Oak shaped leaves and the plant is always erect. Poison Ivy is usually but not always a vine with lateral hairs growing horizontally to cling to trees and walls. Grapevines hang loosely. In winter the Poison Ivy vines turn red. Do not climb on hairy red vines in winter. Poison Sumac is a swamp sumac that grows up to 25 feet with white berries. All of these plants and fruits are eaten by various animals, but are extremely poisonous to man. Avoid all three if possible.

After doing your best trying to avoid these plants you discover that you have just walked through a large patch of Poison Ivy. If you are highly allergic there is still hope of avoiding the allergic reaction. Look first for Jewelweed (Impatiens capensis), also known as impatiens or spotted touch-me-nots. Bruise and rub the stems and leaves directly onto the afflicted area. You can also take a bundle back to camp and make a large kettle of tea from the plants and literally bathe all areas of the body in this warm infusion. This remedy is so effective it has been included in some commercial preparations. Although not nearly as effective, the Jewelweed tea also makes a good after the fact treatment for the poison ivy blisters.

Other remedies include White Willow (Salix alba) bark tea to apply directly to the afflicted area and Wild Lettuce (Lactucca spp.) sap applied to the skin as well.

Native Americans applied Horse Nettle (Solanum carolinense) Tea or poulticed leaves to Poison Ivy rashes. Be careful with this one, as Horse Nettle is an extremely toxic member of the nightshade family and is not related to the stinging nettles. If all else fails, a good scrubbing with soap and water will help prevent the outbreak of the rash once exposed.

Nettles

I remember as a boy running in shorts through chest high weeds down by the creek in southern Indiana and coming out on the other side with red burning welts up and down my legs. These were our good friends the nettles. Specifically, these were Wood-Nettles (Laportea canadensis). The other common nettles that sting include the Stinging Nettle (Utrica dioica) and the Slender Nettle (Utrica gracilis). All of these nettles are highly nutritious edibles as potherbs or as a tea.

At the time I did not know it, but a treatment was also growing all around me as well, in the form of Yellow Dock (Rumex crispus) and Jewelweed. The leaves and stems of either of these two plants can be crushed and rubbed right on the affected area to provide immediate relief.

Curled or Yellow Dock is both edible and medicinal

Assaults from the Animal Kingdom

Many people are put off by the threat presented by bees, ticks, mosquitoes, flies and snakes while in the outdoors. As we increase our awareness, both the fears and the actual assaults diminish rapidly. Nonetheless the mosquitos and flies will continue to bite and the bees will sting on occasion.

Insect Bites and Stings

Whenever I get bitten by a mosquito or stung by a bee, I reach for the nearest Common Plantain (Plantago major), Narrow-leaved Plantain (Plantago lanceolata), or Purslane (Portulaca oleracea). The crushed leaves of any of these plants will give immediate and sustained relief. I usually crush the leaves with my front teeth, as they are all also highly edible. Dr. James Duke suggests that crushed Purslane under the tongue simultaneously applied with crushed purslane on the sting may actually assist with anaphylactic shock. Purslane contains noradrenalin as does the injection provided in an anaphylactic shock kit. He also stresses that the Purslane should be periodically refreshed and to use this only in an emergency, as it has not been clinically validated (CF J/F 94).

Other Wild plants suggested for bee stings and other insect bites include the crushed leaves of Wintercress (Barbarea spp.), sliced root of Wild Onion (Allium vineale), and the inner fleshy side of the split leaves of Prickly Pear Cactus (Opuntia spp.).

Tick Bites

The best way to deal with ticks is to maintain a heightened awareness about your body and eliminate the tick before it becomes imbedded in your skin. Remove the tick as quickly as possible preferably by the head instead of the body, as squeezing his body will tend to flush the contents of her nasty little body into yours. Also ensure you do not leave the head in your flesh. Native Americans used crushed Jimson Weed (Datura Stramonium) on the bites. Warning, Jimson Weed is extremely toxic and may be fatal if ingested, handle with care. Another, much safer remedy is Chestnut (Castanea dentata) paste applied to the wound. Even though the Chestnut blight is here to stay, American Chestnut trees still exist and live long enough to bear nuts. Also any of the hybrid chestnuts will also suffice (Meuninck, 1995).

A Word about Lyme Disease

Recent research indicates that a tick must remain embedded for at least 24 hours before the protein coat of the Lyme Spirochetes can mutate to the infectious state. The protein coat shift can only occur after the gut of the tick has warmed up as a result of its ingestion of warm blood. If you suspect you may have Lyme disease, do not hesitate to seek medical assistance. This disease is easy to treat if detected early, but devastating if allowed to continue. I was treated once for Lyme disease as a precaution and it consisted of a ten-day course of tetracycline or other antibiotic. The good news is that a Lyme vaccine has been submitted to the FDA for approval.

Spider Bites

Smashed Purple Coneflower (Echinacea purpurea) root and Jimson Weed leaves, sliced Prickly Pear leaves sliced in half flesh side down were all used by various Native Americans for spider bites. Again, due to its toxicity, Jimson Weed would be my last choice behind the other two (Meuninck, 1995).

Snake Bites

Chewed leaves and roots of Echinacea placed on the snake bite and Echinacea root tea taken internally were one of the primary Native American treatments for snakebite. A poultice of Jimson Weed leaves placed on a snakebite after sucking. Black Cohosh (Cimicifuga racemosa) root, the precursor to the modern birth control pill, also known as Black Snakeroot, was used for snake bites by Native Americans (Elliot, 1995).

If bitten, try to suck the venom from the bite, either by mouth or preferably with a suction device. Ingestion of snake venom will not hurt you, however it may give you an upset stomach. Open sores in your mouth may present problems. Try to spit out most of the venom in any event.

Do not attempt to cut the snakebite before sucking as this generally results in more damage than from the bite. This is a tradition that needs to become history. Remain calm and seek medical attention as soon as possible.

You may have noticed that several plants seem to dominate the bite treatments. Get to know these few special plants, as they are readily available and extremely versatile medicinals.

The Little Beasties

There are many types of common illnesses the Native Americans and early settlers had to deal with before the advent of modern medicine. Many of the treatments have been incorporated into the modern pharmacopoeia while others have fallen into obscurity. However, as research continues, especially in countries like Germany, more and more herbal remedies are becoming scientifically validated. However, many of the so-called "cures" have also been found to be of no practical use at all. While the jury is still out on some herbal cures, the following treatments have been reported from various sources as effective.

Fungus

Ringworm is not a worm at all, but it is instead a superficial fungal infection. The most common of these include Tinea corpis (ringworm of the body), Tinea pedis (ringworm of the foot, athletes foot), and Tinea cruris (ringworm of the crotch, crotch itch). There are many others that affect specific areas of the body.

Anyone who has experienced any of the above will quickly tells you that only a fungicide is effective on these conditions. Fortunately there are a couple fungicides readily available from nature. Black Walnut (Juglans nigra) hull tea is reported as an effective treatment. Be forewarned, this tea will stain the skin for several days as anyone who has handled them can attest.

Field Garlic (Allium vineale) in particular and other members of the onion family are reported to have significant antifungal properties. Additionally, members of the Monarda family, including Bee Balm (Monarda didyma) are reported to contain the antibacterial agent thymol (Kowalchik, 1987).

The mashed root of Elderberry (Sambucus spp.) provides antifungal action in the treatment of athlete's foot (Meuninck, 1995). Also, a strong tea of Horsetail has been reported as an effective treatment for athlete's foot (Coltsfoot, 1993).

Lice

Pawpaw (Asimina triloba) seeds are reported to contain powerful pediculicides. The application of crushed Pawpaw seeds to affected areas may provide ample treatment (Duke, 1992). Yucca (Yucca filamentosa) Root Shampoo is also reported as an effective treatment (Meuninck, 1995).

Worms

Heal-all (Prunella vulgaris) is reported to be an effective treatment for intestinal worms (Moulton, 1977). Native Americans used pumpkinseeds as a primary treatment for intestinal worms as well.

Heal-All, All-Heal, or Selfheal is good for what ails you

Cold Sores

Goldenseal (Hydrastias canadensis) contains the alkaloid berberine, which may be responsible for its reported efficacy on herpes canker sores. (Tyler, 1994) I have had really good success using a Goldenseal tincture to treat cold sores. Ginseng (Panax quinquefolius) has been widely reported as well as an effective treatment. Burdock Root Tea wash has also been reported as a potent treatment for this malady as well (Heinerman, 1988)

Goldenseal

Warts

Milkweed (Asclepias syriaca) sap has been widely reported as treatment for warts by Native Americans. Crushed Mullein (Verbascum thapsus) flowers have been indicated as an effective treatment (Foster, 1990). A caustic resin, called podophyllin extracted from the Mayapple (Podophyllum peltatum) reportedly works well on some warts (Elliot, 1995).

Milkweed

Coughs

No other herb has a longer history as a cough remedy than Coltsfoot (Tussilago farfara), however, recent studies suggest this herb may be dangerous or perhaps carcinogenic. There is evidence to the contrary about the carcinogenic nature from human chromosome studies and it is still considered safe by doctors in Germany for short-term use (Castleman, 1991).

Pioneers used a strong combination of Red Clover (Trifolium pratense), onion juice and strained honey to relieve whooping cough spasms (McPherson, 1977).

Elderberry (Sambucus canadense) juice and Wild Ginger (Asarum canadense) tea have also been widely reported as cough remedies. A tea made from Violet (Viola spp.) leaves and flowers is reported to have strong expectorant action as well.

Coltsfoot

Bacterial Infections

Blueberries (Vaccinium spp.) are reported to attack E. coli in the stomach. (Meuninck, 1992) Garlic has a long and incredible history for its ability to fight internal and external infection and the scientific validation to back it up. Garlic was used extensively during WWII, as wound antiseptic in Great Britain with no reported cases of infection. Wild Garlic (Allium canadense) and Field Garlic (Allium vineale) contain the same active ingredients and are readily available in the wild.

Wild Ginger (Asarum canadense) has also been found to contain two active antibiotic substances (Elliot, 1995).

Nausea/Motion Sickness

Most members of the mint and chamomile family have been recommended for soothing an upset stomach. However, the active property found in both domestic and Wild Ginger have proven to be significantly more effective than over-the-counter medications without the drowsy side effects (Carper, 1997).

Diarrhea

Diarrhea may be treated with a Sunflower (Helianthus annuus) leaf tea made by steeping one teaspoon of sunflower leaves in one cup of water for 10 -minutes. Use one half to one teaspoon according to age. Caution needs to be taken as an overdose may stop bowel action for two to three days (Moulton, 1993).

Native Americans used Mulberries (Morus spp.) to treat dysentery as well as using Blackberry (Rubus spp.) root bark (Meuninck, 1990). A common folk medicine treatment can be made from a tea made from the seeds of Plantain (Plantago spp) (Readers Digest, 1986).

A protozoan called Giardia lamblia can create a condition known as Giardia from drinking water infected from feces of animals. This protozoan can be found in the most pristine of environments with sparkling clean water. In fact, the higher the concentration of wildlife, the more likely it will be found. One of the many symptoms of this infection includes diarrhea, but it is often difficult to diagnose. Treating the diarrhea alone in the case of giardia is not enough; the protozoa must be destroyed as well.

Sunflower

Constipation

Psyllium seed is the active ingredient in some natural over-the-counter laxatives. This seed comes from a member of the Plantain family called Plantago psyllium. Other members of this family include Common Plantain (Plantago major) and Narrow-leaf Plantain (Plantago lanceolata). The psyllium seeds from these two species may also be used as well.

Mullein (Verbascum thapsus) leave tea also makes a very effective and mild laxative. I have tried this tea more for its culinary attributes, but found it to be a mild, yet effective laxative. Mullein leaves contain rotenone and coumarin and both are on the not recommended list with the FDA (WFF J/A, 1995). Aloe vera tablets are sold in health food stores as a mild laxative as well.

Eating an excessive amount of Day-lily stalks may thoroughly clean-out the plumbing, as myself and a couple of other overambitious Day-lily connoisseurs discovered during a wild edible course.

My son with a large Mullein plant

Hemorrhoids

Poultices from fresh and dried Mullein are also reported to be an effective hemorrhoid treatment.

Eye Problems

Goldenseal root was the preferred treatment for eye problems by the Cherokee Indians and has been the predominant herbal treatment for eye problems for over one hundreds years. The Iroquois used Goldenseal as a remedy for a whole list of maladies. Goldenseal possesses significant antibiotic and antiseptic properties. Use a cooled infusion made by steeping roots in freshly boiled water for treatment. The bright yellow Goldenseal preparations usually stain the skin yellow, hence the other common name Yellow Root.

Ear Aches

Mullein flowers soaked in an oil base are reported to make an effective ear drop treatment for ear infections.

Flu and Colds

Eat garlic everyday and eat lots of garlic when you get sick. Garlic contains many natural antibiotics. Field Garlic specifically and Wild Garlic are both readily available in nature throughout much of the United States.

Purple Coneflower (Echinacea pupurea) and Pale Purple Coneflower (Echinacea pallida) have been proven effective for the treatment of cold and flu symptoms in German studies. All parts of the plant are considered effective. I will often begin taking Echinacea when I feel the onset of a cold or flu along with increased garlic intake. Usually this will prevent the viruses from taking hold. Although anecdotal evidence like this is not proof of efficacy, it works for me.

Asian Ginger (Zingiber offinale) has shown significant efficacy on rhinoviruses (Duke, 1997). Although Wild Ginger (Asarum canadense) is not related to Asian Ginger it contains many similar biochemical properties and may prove effective as well.

An Algerian born, Israeli scientist studying for her PhD in Switzerland discovered two chemical compounds found in Elderberry (Sambucus nigra) juice which prevent flu viruses from invading throat cells. In her research she discovered that 90 percent of the patients given an extract from the juice at the first sign of fever felt well within three days as opposed to six days for the control group (Castleman, 1995).

Depression

Saint John's Wort (Hypericum perforatum) made national headlines during 1997 as a potential superior remedy for treating some forms of depression. Anecdotal testimony from many individuals has corroborated recent European studies touting the efficacy of the herb in treating depression. The National Institutes of Health (NIH) was so impressed by the positive results indicated by the European studies, they are considering funding further studies in the United States.

Stimulants

In the classical use of the word "stimulants" there is only one predominant North American wild herb that qualifies, Mormon Tea (Ephedra nevadensis). This is the same plant mentioned for decongestion, containing three strong central nervous system stimulants; ephedrine, pseudoephedrine, and norpseudoephedrine (Castleman, 1991). As the common and scientific names suggest, this plant occurs naturally only in the southwestern United States.

In another use of the word "stimulant", to stimulate the organs there are several other plants that fit the bill. Most of the mints (Mentha spp.) have a stimulating effect on the gastrointestinal tract. The Maidenhair Tree (Ginkgo biloba), most often referred to as Ginkgo, has been shown in several studies to significantly increase blood flow throughout the body. The increased blood flow has been attributed to increased memory and cognitive abilities as well as alertness. It is also said to increase libido as blood flow increases to both the sexual organs and the brain. The active ingredients from Ginkgo are derived from its leaves. However, due to the high tannin content and the large quantities required for effectiveness, drinking the tea alone may not be enough to obtain positive results.

Sedatives

Valerian was found to be an effective sedative and antianxiety remedy with no side effects. The powerful pharmacological sleeping pill Halcion, and antianxiety drug Xanax both were reported to have undesirable side effects. Halcion side effects include hangovers and loss of concentration, while Xanax is strongly addictive. Valerian was as effective as either drug and safer than both with no significant side effects (Carper, 1997). Motherwort (Leonurus caradiaca) has been shown to be a mild sedative similar to Valerian in German studies (Castleman, 1991).

Lemon Balm (Melissa officinalis) has also been recommended in Germany as a superior sleep inducer (Duke, 1997). Yarrow contains a hypnotic chemical called thujone, which in small amounts may have a similar effect as marijuana. In large quantities thujone is poison. Yarrow has a history of traditional use as a sedative (Castleman, 1991).

Two other plants that thrive in wet hardwood forests with natural sedative action include Wild Oats (Avena sativa) and Violet (Viola odorata).

Keeping Healthy

It is no big secret that watching one's diet combined with regular exercise is the key to good health. Mother Nature can help in a big way here, as some of these most nutritious fruits and vegetables are found in nature and not in the grocery store. Modern fruits and vegetables have been cultivated and manipulated for marketability as their primary traits. These traits include economy, transportability, shelf life, appearance and flavor. Nutritional value is not included in the list. Flavor is optional and is second to all the other traits.

Nutrition Enhancers

Dandelion (Taraxacum offinale) is the overall king of nutrition in nature. These escaped cultivars were brought over as a food source from Europe. With its abundant mobile parachute seeds, it rapidly spread throughout the continent. Dandelion is still heavily cultivated in Europe, particularly in France, Spain, Italy and Portugal, but not so much here. Vineland, NJ has seized the title as the Dandelion capital of North America. Vineland grows more "wild type" dandelions for commercial marketing than any other town in North America. Mostly ethnic minorities from the aforementioned countries purchase these.

How nutritious is dandelion? Here is a comparison to some of the well known highly nutritious vegetables:

	Protein	Cal	Ca	Iron	K	A	Vit Ribo	Vit C
Dandelion	2.7	45	187	3.1	397	14000	.16	80
Broccoli	2.98	32	103	1.1	325	2500	.23	113
Spinach	3.2	26	93	3.1	558	8100	.20	51
Lettuce (iceberg)	1.3	13	20	.5	150	330	.06	6[1]

---

1. Protein measured in grams, calcium in mg, iron in mg, potassium in mg, vitamin A in International Units, riboflavin in mg, and vitamin C in mg.

As you can see the nutritional content is significantly more robust in the dandelion than in any of its domestic counterparts. The above listings are just a sampling of its nutritional constituents. Other constituent comparisons are equally impressive.

Dandelion has also been touted as a miracle herb that can cure or prevent a list of maladies including liver diseases, poor vision, obesity, lower blood pressure, lower cholesterol, cancer prevention and treatment, and diabetes prevention and treatment (Gail, 1994). Another natural plant that has been credited with relieving adult-onset diabetes is Prickly Pear Cactus (Opuntia spp.). There has also been some scientific validation of this claim as well (Nyerges, 1997).

Other readily available superfoods in nature include Nettles (Utrica dioica), Amaranth (Amaranths spp.), Lamb's-quarters (Chenopodium album), and Violets (Viola spp.). Again compare the nutritional values with common vegetables.

	Protein	Cal	Ca	Iron	K	A	Vit Ribo	Vit C
Nettles	6.9	---	---	---	---	6566	---	76
Amaranth	2.1	26	215	2.3	50	2917	.16	43
Lambsquarters	4.2	43	309	1.2	0	11600	.44	80
Violets	----	--	----	---	---	8200	----	210
Orange	.94	47	40	.1	181	205	.04	53.2
Broccoli	2.98	32	103	1.1	325	2500	.23	113
Spinach	3.2	26	93	3.1	558	8100	.20	51
Lettuce(iceberg)	1.3	13	20	.5	150	330	.06	6[1]

Not only are the wild plants generally more nutritious, they are also 100% organic. Assuming the forager is careful, they are free of herbicides, pesticides and pollutants.

High Blood Pressure

Besides changing your diet and exercise habits, Mother Nature may provide assistance for lowering high blood pressure. The American Linden Tree (Tilia americana), also known as the Basswood Tree, has been linked to the lowering of blood pressure. Field Garlic, Feverfew (Chrysanthemum parthenium), Plantain seeds, and Nettles have all been suggested as effective agents to lower blood pressure as well. Stinging Nettle is prescribed in Germany as a safe and effective diuretic (Castleman, 1991). Bee Balm has been reported to contain powerful flavanoids to lower blood pressure (Meuninck, 1995).

High Cholesterol

Garlic leads the list as a primary force in lowering high cholesterol. Look for Field Garlic and Wild Garlic in waste places and fields. This highly concentrated form of garlic is high in allicin, the active ingredient in Garlic thought to be responsible for most of its therapeutic properties.

Like its unrelated domestic namesake, Wild Ginger may have significant cholesterol reducing ability. Sweetflag (Acorus calamus) contains choline, an anticholesterol phytochemical (Harris,

---

1. Protein measured in grams, calcium in mg, iron in mg, potassium in mg, vitamin A in International Units, riboflavin in mg, and vitamin C in mg.

1971). Recent research indicates that eating foods high in Omega-3 fatty acids significantly reduces cholesterol levels. Purslane (Portulaca oleracea), an imported escapee from early European immigrants, has the highest level of omega-3 fatty acids of any other leafy plant source. This plant is found growing wild throughout most of North America (Meuninck, 1995).

Immune Enhancers/Adaptogens

There are two immune enhancers that have been widely used and reported to contain phytochemicals that boost the immune system, Goldenseal and Purple Coneflower (Echinacea spp.). While the scientific jury is still out on Goldenseal, Echinacea has been researched and documented extensively. This is particularly true in Germany where they have over two hundred and fifty drugs containing Echinacea as an active ingredient (Foster, 1991). Although Goldenseal has not enjoyed the same endorsement from the mainstream medical field, there is an abundance of anecdotal evidence that it also is an effective immune enhancer.

Another herb available in the wild, Heal-All (Prunella vulgaris), also known as Self-heal and All-heal, has been suggested as an effective immune enhancer. It contains very high levels of antioxidants (Duke, 1997). Another widely available wild medicinal herb with immune enhancing potential is the Saint John's Wort (Hypericum perforatum). Saint John's Wort demonstrated significant antiviral activity in a 1988 New York University study on a family of viruses including Human Immunodeficiency Virus (HIV). Ginger has also shown promise as an immune enhancer as well (Castleman, 1991). Today grape seed extract is leading the pack as one of the most potent superantioxidant sources available. Grape seed extract is sold in health food stores across the country, but it is also available in the form of raw grape seeds that can be collected from nature for free.

Russian scientists who conducted extensive research on Siberian Ginseng (Eleutherococus senticosus) coined the term "adaptogen". The research they conducted was extensive but not very rigorous. Their methods were sometimes sloppy and undisciplined, so their conclusions are suspect by much of the scientific community. However, enough of the research and lots of folklore do suggest there may be something to the claims of Ginseng.

A related species of a different genus, American Ginseng (Panax quinquefolius) can be found growing wild in wet hardwood forests east of the Mississippi. Although these species are not closely related, they share remarkably similar phytochemicals that may have the same pharmaceutical effect. The main constituents thought to be responsible for Ginseng's remarkable abilities are a class of saponins called ginsenosides. A more closely related Ginseng, Oriental Ginseng (Panax ginseng) contains an even more similar set of ginsenosides, but only in smaller concentrations than that found in American Ginseng. This is the main reason that American Ginseng brings the highest prices in the world, at times greater than $500 a pound.

What Ginseng is supposed to do for your health forms an exhaustive list. Just about anything that could be described to make body adapt to varying conditions for peak efficiency is attributed to Ginseng. Near the top of the descriptive list are the terms: aphrodisiac, life extender, radiation sickness, tonic, immune enhancer, cancer prevention and cure, and the list goes on. There has probably been more written about this group of herbs than any other. More research has been conducted on Ginseng than any other herb, although most of the research was not considered "good" science. Recently there has been more promising indications that Ginseng probably is the real thing, but the Western jury is still out on this one. The oriental cultures including the Chinese, Japanese and Koreans need no convincing. They swear by it. Can two billion people be wrong?

Chapter 10: Natural Pest Controls

"When you are close to nature you can listen to the voice of God."

Hermann Hesse

One aspect of adapting to the Wilderness is dealing with the flies, ticks and mosquitoes and other hungry natives. Several years ago I was on a daylight visit to the Everglades National Park, walking on a highly vegetated trail segment. Whenever I paused to take in the scenery, every inch of my bare skin immediately became covered with tiger mosquitoes. I did not bring any commercial or herbal insect repellents. I was not expecting to be assaulted in broad daylight by mosquitoes. The Osage Indians had to cope with this problem as well. The way Native Americans dealt with this was by some of the means listed below and also through diet. Their diet was a low-fat, high fiber, and vitamin and mineral rich. This renders the human body all but tasteless to most pests. The opposite diet makes humans a feeding station beacon.

Diet

The dietary constituents most widely viewed as having a natural repellent effect are the complex B vitamins along with allicin and related components found in garlic and onions. Eat lots of greens such as Lamb's-quarters (Chenopodium album), Dandelion (Taraxacum officinale), and Sunflower (Helianthus annuus) seeds for very high vitamin B content. Eat garlic and onion, both domestic and wild for allicin and related components. Wild Garlic (Allium canadense) and Field Garlic (Allium vineale) contain the same active ingredients and are readily available in the wild.

There are certain foods to avoid as well. These include nuts, peanuts, peanut butter, bananas, and caffeine. Caffeine products include caffeinated coffee, teas, sodas and chocolate. Don't forget that most of those delicious trail mixes contain ample amounts of bananas, nuts, and chocolate chips. All of these foods enhance your body's attractiveness to insect pests.

Diet is the first weapon against natural pests, but this may be the most difficult to attain in our modern world without total immersion into the wilderness experience. Luckily there is a great deal more available in our arsenal of natural defenses we can use.

Biological Warfare

The plant kingdom's rich biodiversity is an endless source of sophisticated solutions to nature's challenges and often our own. Chemical warfare was not invented by man, but by nature and it is all around us. Take for example the Black Walnut Tree (Juglans nigra). You may notice that not many plants can grow well within the drip line of this tree. This is because the black walnut tree has a very powerful herbicide, that is released from the roots and the soft outer hull of the nuts called juglone. Juglone also has other beneficial characteristics besides its' herbicidal properties as we will see later. Usually when a plant has a strong odor, it is either trying to repel predators or attract pollinators or both. We are looking for predator repellents that will repel insects that pester humans as well.

Probably the most well known and least objectionable repellents come from the mint family (Labiatea) where there are 160 Genera and 3200 species (Britton, 1970). These repellents are effective against mosquitos, flies, fleas, and ticks. Most of the strongly mint scented plants have a degree of efficacy, but Pennyroyal (Hedeoma pulegioide and Mentha pulegium) and Citronelle (Collinsonia canadensis) provide some of the strongest repellents in nature. The prominent ethnobotanist, Dr. Duke, recommends Mountain Mint (Pycnanthemum muticum) as one of the most effective natural bug repellents (Duke, 1997). As with most natural repellents, the crushed mint leaves are applied directly on the skin or clothes. Another method is to brew them into a strong tea also known as a wash and then apply. Warning, Pennyroyal tea has been linked to severe liver damage after moderate consumption. Both Pennyroyal and Mountain Mint should be avoided at all times by pregnant women as they may induce miscarriages. Eucalyptus is another powerful repellent, but the range of this Australian immigrant in North America is not as wide spread as the mints.

Feverfew (Chrysanthemum parthenium) a naturalized escapee from Europe with a wide range throughout North America contains the insecticidal compound called Pyrethrin that is commercially obtained from Pyrethrum (Chrysanthemum cinraiifolium). Make a wash of the dried tops of the feverfew plants into a powerful insecticide. Do not ingest. This is not an insect repellent but an insect killer that is highly effective (Grainger, 1991). Use this potent poison with caution around humans.

Other repellents especially effective against flies and mosquitos are made from a wash of the roots of Bloodroot (Sanguinaria canadensis). Be very careful with this highly toxic tea. Goldenseal root (Hydrastis canadensis) infused into bear grease and elderberries (Sambucus canadensis) root salve are also said to be effective repellents. A cooled wash of crushed and boiled leaves of Mayapple (Podophyllum peltatum) also makes a natural repellent. These concoctions are applied to the skin and clothing. These compounds may stain clothes and skin alike and are all poisonous if ingested (Meuninck, 1995).

Another pest, ringworm, which is not really a worm at all, but a fungus, can be effectively treated with a wash made from the outer hulls of black walnuts. This wash is equally effective on other fungi such as athlete's foot. This wash will definitely stain your skin for several days, if not weeks, but it will work.

Osage-Orange (Maclura pomifera) fruit may be an effective bug repellent for keeping pests, particularly roaches, away from dwellings or storage places. Place the odiferous fruits on the floor in any area you wish to protect. This fruit is not edible by humans although cattle and horses do eat them.

If your camp or dwelling is near a water hole that is a producer of mosquitoes try to locate some Sweetflag (Acorus Calamus) from another location to transplant into the mosquito producing water. Mosquito larvae cannot exist in the presence of the aromatic cattail look-alike (Gibbons, 1971). Calamus contains an insect chemosterilant called acoric acid. Calamus root can also be used in place of mothballs in the home.

Gardens

There are many natural pest controls that can be applied to gardens in order to keep insect damage to a minimum. Although the applications presented here are all natural and organic, do not be lulled into a false sense of security. Just because they are organic does not mean they are also safe for ingestion. However, being organic makes them mostly water soluble and biodegradable.

The crushed boiled leaves of the toxic Mayapple make an effective insect spray for the garden. This one should probably be limited to the non-edible garden. Another effective spray for the non-edible garden can be made from an extract of Larkspurs and Delphiniums (Meuninck, 1995).

Any of the saponin containing plants such as Yucca can be used to make a soapy solution for direct application on edible gardens (see section on soaps). Powdered Pawpaw bark contains many natural insecticidal compounds. Many of these insecticides have not yet been fully explored by the scientific community.

Other Pest controls

There is a couple of other pest controls worth mentioning primarily for folklore value. As interesting as these are, their efficacy is dubious. Native Americans used Evening Primrose to attract deer and ward off snakes. They also placed Juniper bows around their bedrolls to ward off snakes. Buttercups were used by Native Americans to ward off bears. (Meuninck, 1995).

Chapter 11: Nature's Bag of Tricks

"Good architecture lets nature in."

Mario Pei

The Bow Drill

The Bow Drill is the most versatile of all the natural fire starting apparatuses. It is one of the easiest to use to start a fire with and the components are readily available year round. There are six basic components that make up the bow drill: tinder, handhold, bow, bowstring, drill (spindle), and fireboard.

Make **Tinder** from dry, highly flammable, dead plant materials. Buff and shred this material to a light fluffy state before using. Pull jute string apart to make artificial tinder. Choose one of the tinder sources listed under *Sources for Tinder*.

The **Handhold** is a small piece of wood that fits comfortably in your hand. The choice of wood for this piece is not critical. Drill a socket into the handhold before adding lubrication to the handhold or the drill as described in the method below.

The **Bow** is a long piece of wood measured from armpit to fingers outstretched, slightly bowed. Use the bow level and close to the ground with rapid full strokes.

The **Bowstring** is any cordage around 1/8" thick that is strong enough to use with the bow drill. Make cordage from natural fibers or use a parachute cord or other small diameter rope.

The **Drill or Spindle** is the other moving part of the bow drill. Make the drill from select dry hardwoods. The drill is 8 to 10 inches long and about 1 inch in diameter or the size of a quarter. Carve one end to a steep point, the other to a rounded point. Carve a ring around the circumference of the drill about one inch from the round end to ensure the two ends are not mixed up. Lubricate the rounded end using soap, pine pitch, oil from the side of your nose, or oil from the hair on your head. Add the lubricant only after the socket has been burned into the handhold. Keep the other end absolutely dry and clean. Use either a dead, dry (but not rotten limb) for the spindle or carve it from a solid chunk of wood. Choose one of the woods listed under *Sources for Drill and Fireboards*.

Make the **Fireboard** from select dry hardwood that is flat on the bottom and the top. The dimensions are 3/4 to 1 inch thick, 8 to 12 inches long and at least twice the width of the drill. Choose one of the woods listed under *Sources for Drill and Fireboards*. A socket must be drilled into the fireboard about 1/4 of an inch away from the edge. Cut a notch from the edge of the fireboard to just shy of the center of the socket.

Method

To use the bow drill, place the tinder on a dry surface off the ground on a piece of bark or other dry material. Place the fireboard so the notch is over the center of the tinder. Twist the spindle through the bowstring so the spindle is on the outside of the string and bow. Make sure it is tight. Place the non-lubricated end of the bow into the fireboard socket and the lubricated end into the handhold socket. If you are right-handed, place your left foot securely onto the end of the fireboard and kneel on the right knee. Grasp the handhold with the left hand and securely anchor the left hand against the left leg. This step is very important to prevent your arm from wearing out and the drill from wobbling. Lean over the left hand and handhold so your chest is centered over the bow drill. This will also protect your apparatus from rain and allow you to easily apply downward pressure to create the necessary friction.

Begin to make long, level, rapid strokes close to the ground. It may be necessary to grab some bowstring with your bow hand to tighten the string as you progress. When thick white smoke begins to appear, make ten more vigorous strokes to ensure a good coal has formed.

Set the handhold, drill, and bow aside. Carefully push the coal downward by placing a knife point at the apex of the notch and roll the fireboard away from the coal. Cradle the coal in the center of the tender and begin to blow steadily into the coal. Do not hold the tinder and coal above your head as the coal may roll out and burn your eyes. If necessary, compress the tinder as you blow. As more smoke forms blow harder until the tinder ignites. Practice, practice, and practice until you get it to work. Once you get it to work, it is like riding a bike; you will not forget.

Sources for Drill and Fireboards

Best
Cottonwood and Willows

Good
Aspens (all)
Alder
Birch
Beech
Sycamore
Sumac
Sassafras
Sage
Mesquite
Basswood
Elder
Fruitwoods (any)
Juniper
Redwood

Fair - Very hard woods - need small thin materials
Oaks
Hickories
Walnuts
*Cedar

Avoid - Resinous woods
Pines
Spruces
Firs

*This is the only wood that works wet.

Sources of Tender

Dead Inner Bark
Cedar*
Willow
Cottonwood
Aspen
Basswood
Elm
Walnut*
Cherry
Hickory
Oak*
Sage
Box Elder
Ash

Plant Outer Fibers
Nettles*
Velvetleaf (Indian Mallow)
Dogbane*
Milkweed
Fireweed
Yucca
Primrose

Must mix filler plant downs
(mix no more than 1/3 volume)

Cattail
Thistle
Milkweed
Dogbane
Dandelion
Cotton Sedge

* Works better mixed with other fibers

Author lighting a fire with his bow drill

Basketry

Willow baskets have become an icon for the Native American lifestyle. However, basketry was made from many different plant sources in addition to willow. Barks from various trees, like Birch, Tulip Poplar, and others make fantastic baskets. Vines such as Grape, Virginia Creeper, Briers, and others make great baskets as well. Long leafed plants such as Cattail, Sedges, Sweetflag, and others also make great basket material. Learn a few simple basket-making skills from local basketry groups. Once you have made your first few simple baskets, you will be free to experiment with a vast assortment of natural materials available free in nature.

Pine Pitch Glue

Among the many innovations of the Native Americans was pine pitch glue. Pine pitch glue is a natural two-part glue much like modern epoxy. Pine pitch is pine tree sap and the activator or catalyst is either egg shell, mollusk shell, or ash. The efficacy of pine pitch glue is primarily dependent upon the purity of the pitch and activator as well as the choice of activator.

The most readily available source of pitch is that which is visible on pine trees. This pitch is generally white or amber in color and has other discoloration due to the presence of bugs, bark, dust and other impurities. This sap that contains these impurities is usually sufficient for most applications, but is nonetheless, the least desirable. Filtering sap through natural filters produces the next best quality of pitch. Filtering materials include grass leaves, which is one of the most readily available natural filter sources. This will generally require melting the pitch as this old pitch is generally in solid form. The highest quality pitch is obtained from a fresh wound or a tap fresh from the tree. Spiles for tapping trees for sap can be made from short sections of pipe or tubing. Natural spiles can be made from plant stems with pithy centers, such as Elder and Reed Grass.

Firewood ash is a sufficient activator for most applications; however, it is the least desirable in the pecking order of activator choices. Wood ash is simply the dry whitish gray fluffy residue from burning wood. Judiciously avoid any wet or soggy ash, as this is now highly concentrated and caustic lye that will burn the skin on contact. The next higher caliber of activator is finely ground mollusk shell. This can be from any mollusk, freshwater clamshells, saltwater clamshells, land snail shells etc. Ensure the shell is ground finely to a powder. The more finely ground the better the activator will work. The highest quality activator is made from finely ground eggshell. Again this can be from any source of bird eggshell, from chicken to ostrich.

The glue is used by first applying the liquid pitch to the surface to be glued. In the case of unrefined solid pitch, it will first have to be melted with fire. After the liquid pitch is applied a fine dusting of the surface with the activator will instantly harden the glue. If heat was used in the application, cooling will further harden the glue.

Pine pitch glue is a great all around glue and can be used in many applications. I have found that Pine Pitch Glue tends to melt if it is exposed to high heat like very hot soup in a wooden bowl. This may produce a very piney taste in your food.

Repairing a bowl with pine pitch glue

Shelters

Wickiup: A Shelter for All Seasons

The wickiup {pronounced Wick ee up} was a shelter used by various Native Americans. A Wickiup is basically a stationary Teepee made from sticks or logs, debris, and sometimes hides, blankets or other coverings. They ranged in size from small one or two man affairs, to very large structures that could accommodate several dozen people. Some were very temporary while others were long term shelters. The smaller wickiups are more suitable for milder weather unless you bring sleeping bags to keep warm. A very small fire in a small wickiup can be used, but must be constantly attended. Hot rocks from an open fire far from the Wickiup would be a much safer choice. A larger Wickiup with a fire pit, safety zone, fire barrier, and high roof is a better choice for year round living and significantly safer as well.

Family members and myself built a large permanent year round structure. It required several days to construct with two and sometimes three people working together. A wickiup of this size should not be considered for short term or emergency use.

To build a Wickiup you must first select a site where the building materials are plentiful. Primary building materials include long logs or sticks with sufficient diameter and strength to support the size of the structure and lots of debris. If you are building a wickiup six feet in diameter probably sticks of forearm diameter will be sufficient. If you are building one twenty-three feet in diameter, as the one pictured here, your first course of logs will be six to eight inches or more. You do not need to kill many, if any trees to build a Wickiup. During the construction of this wickiup we only used two live trees in the beginning to obtain the proper forks to lock the logs together. If you do need to cut any living trees, adopt the earth caretaker attitude of the Native Americans when selecting the trees. Select trees that are sick, unhealthy or in overcrowded growing conditions that will enhance the overall wood stand.

If you have a selection of wood types to use, pick strong woods that will hold up well in outdoor conditions, fence post type woods. These include black locust, cedar, oak, osage orange, walnut etc. The more rot resistant the wood, the longer it will last.

Before selecting a site for a wickiup, decide how the wickiup will be used and what the floor plan will look like. The wickiup pictured was designed to have a three-foot fire pit, three-foot safety zone, log barrier and about an eight foot wide sleeping ring. What resulted was a floor about twenty five feet in diameter.

Select a relatively flat area free of any trees larger than saplings. Cut a piece of cordage to the desired radius length and peg it to the middle of your Wickiup site. Mark a circle around the site using the pegged cordage as your guide. Once this is completed, do a little quick math or guesstimate to get approximately a 45-degree angle and then make the poles longer so the angle is greater. If you do not want to use math, just make sure the rise is shorter than run so that the debris won't roll off. Add even more length so the poles will cross at the top. The one pictured is about twelve feet high inside with about four feet of pole overlap. Remember the top of the wickiup will not be covered, just like in a teepee. This opening will serve as the smoke hole and will help cool the shelter in the summer.

Begin construction by erecting and interlocking the first three logs. This will probably take at least one forked log. These logs should be some of the heaviest logs used in the project, as they will form the foundation for all that follow.

After the first three logs are securely in place, begin filling in the gaps. As the empty space begins to fill, choose a site for the door between two sturdy supports of appropriate distance apart.

At this point you need to start thinking about how you will keep the debris from falling through the door. This usually involves erecting some uprights or using logs in the doorway that have perpendicular limbs attached. During the construction of this Wickiup we used upright poles and lashed a pole across the two. A ridge pole was attached to the cross poles and then to two uprights about six feet out from the entrance forming a V. To complete this igloo type door, ribs were laid from the ridge pole to the ground on both sides.

An eastern facing door is preferable in most instances to take advantage of the morning sun and to avoid the worst of the bad weather, which usually comes from the west in most of the United States. Continue adding logs until most of the empty space has been filled. At this point you may optionally add a covering of some sort which may include, skins, bark, blankets, plastic, etc. This extra covering will provide additional insulation and fire protection against sparks, but is not required.

Debris will provide the insulation, wind, and water proofing. Pile the debris, which includes forest litter, grasses, bark and anything else that creates loft and dead air space. The debris on the outside should be at least three feet deep for all weather protection all the way up to where the poles open up at the top. Place light limbs on top of the debris to keep them from blowing away. Do not use limbs that are too heavy as they will compress the loft and decrease dead air space.

On the inside dig a fire pit about three feet wide and one foot deep. Line the top of the fire pit with rocks. Completely clear a three-foot ring all the way around the fire pit. Next make a ring around the safety zone with rocks or logs. Try to make the barrier at least six inches high. Eighteen-inch logs placed upright were used in this Wickiup to make the ring and led all the way to the door. On the outside of the barrier ring place one to two feet of debris for insulation and sleeping comfort.

A thatched door may be constructed or a piece of tanned hide, blanket or burlap can be used. When using the firepit, always make a tepee fire to ensure it is relatively smokeless. Also keep the fire small and never leave unattended while still in the blazing state.

This is a great shelter for communal living and working. It serves well as a hunting cabin and meeting place. Whenever possible add more debris to the outside and inside. With minimal maintenance this shelter will serve you well and long.

Debris Hut

The Debris Hut is a true four-season, all weather shelter. Under ideal conditions, it can be constructed in less than one hour. This shelter can protect you from driving rains, sleet or snow and can mean the difference between life and death from hypothermia in temperatures well below freezing. If properly constructed this shelter will keep you dry during torrential rains. Native Americans and many other primitive peoples from around the world used the Debris Hut. Whether you are looking for an emergency shelter, short-term shelter, or a means to camp without the use of a sleeping bag and tent, there is no other natural shelter as versatile. Native Americans often traveled great distances with nothing, more than a loin cloth and primitive knife and wanted for nothing including shelter.

There is nothing particularly magical about the Debris Hut other than its simplicity and efficacy. In a word, it is nothing more than an orderly bunch of sticks and forest debris. There are, however, some very exacting guidelines for making the Debris Hut work. It is very important to make and sleep in your first Debris Hut in a controlled, but challenging environment. Before totally abandoning a sleeping bag and tent try a Debris Hut under controlled conditions. Test your skills where you have a back-up place to sleep as you learn the lessons of the Debris Hut. Preferably you can build a Debris Hut right before it rains and with good planning right before it gets too cold and wet. This experience will teach you lessons that you will never forget. Most first attempts will be totally or partially successful. If you follow the guidelines presented, you will be successful. Your learning experience will be that of total confidence in your ability to build a good Debris Hut. If you are partially successful you will quickly discover what you did wrong and usually you can correct the deficiency quickly. If you totally miss the mark, you will discover your mistakes in very short order as well.

Take the following guidelines literally. Once you become experienced you may vary the routine according to the situation, but at least on the first try stick to the rules. When the guidelines call for three feet of debris, it does not mean three inches, it means three feet.

The three most important factors for deciding the value of real estate are location, location, location; so too for the Debris Hut. A transition area is the upscale location for our shelter. A transition area is a location where different biomes meet, like woods and field or field and water. For our purposes we are specifically looking for the woods to field transition area. This transition area will provide an abundance of building materials and ample morning sun to help warm up things. Structural building materials such as the ridgepole and ribbing and cross-hatching will come from the woods. The other major type of building material, debris, will come from both woods and the field. Debris will form our insulation and water proofing.

The last aspect of location is orientation. Cold and rainy weather in eastern United States generally comes from the west. The entrance should face the east on the western side of a transition area if possible. This will also take advantage of the warming morning sun as well.

Once a location has been selected it is time to find a support and ridgepole of sufficient length and strength. The support for the ridgepole should be about crotch high. A stump makes a good support as do full-grown trees or a smaller tree with a fork at the appropriate height. When using a full-grown tree, jam the ridgepole firmly into the tree at the appropriate height.

A freestanding support is constructed from two poles driven in the ground at an angle to hold the ridgepole where they come together. These sticks should be forked or tethered to hold the ridgepole. Remember to make the doorway at the support large enough to squeeze into, but no larger. This is very important to minimize heat loss. Think of the Debris Hut more as a giant sleeping bag, rather than a tent.

The ridgepole should be at least the diameter of your forearm. It should be of sufficient length such that when you lay under the supported ridgepole you can move your feet freely from side to side. If the ridgepole is not long enough, a rock or a log placed under the foot end may solve the problem. Mark the debris hut width with your hands about three inches outside your shoulder width while on the ground measuring the ridge pole length.

Gather the ribbing from available sticks in the area. The majority of the ribbing should be at least wrist size in diameter, but this can vary. Ensure the ribbing sticks are free of perpendicular limbs and do not extend beyond the ridgepole more than three inches. Both artifacts will channel water into the interior and make it very difficult to seal. Stagger the ribbing from the support down to the base. You do not need to get the ribbing contiguous, but the closer together the better. Follow the marked outline from the door to the foot. Taper in as you head toward the foot always allowing at least three inches on either side of your body for ample room.

Upon completion of the ribbing, collect small limbs to place horizontally and at angles to the ribbing. The purpose of the cross-hatching is to keep the debris from passing through the ribs. Once you have placed enough cross hatching on the shelter it is time for the debris.

Debris is any forest or field litter, such as leaves, pine needles, grass, etc. The loftier the better. The goal here is to create dead air space just like down in a jacket. Use a blanket, coat, poncho or anything else available to gather larger amounts of debris at a time. If these items are not available, use your hands. Pile debris on the shelter until you have two to three feet or more. For colder conditions use more. Use less debris during milder or hotter weather. Three feet is approximately the length of your arm. The debris is three feet thick when your arm is shoulder deep in the debris while touching the ribs. If you cannot reach the ribs then this is even better. Double check from the inside to make sure no light comes through. If you see light make an extra effort to ensure you totally plug it up. Less debris can be used by sandwiching layers of sticks between layers of debris as follows: six-inches of debris; six-inches of sticks, six-inches of debris, six-inches of sticks and six-inches of debris. This uses only a total of eighteen inches of debris and twelve inches of sticks.

When the debris is sufficiently thick, then place enough light limbs on top to ensure the debris will not blow away. This will also help prevent the debris from settling to the base of the Debris Hut. Make sure these limbs are not too heavy, as this may compress the debris and eliminate the loft.

Upon completion of the exterior, collect debris for the interior of the shelter. First stuff the foot area solid and then the base of the interior along the sides. For extra warmth, eliminate the roof angle. Use small cross members about three or four inches from the top and stuff full of debris. Choose the softest and most comfortable debris for the rest of the interior, as this will come in direct contact with your body. The debris does not have to be dry either on the outside or inside of the shelter. Wet debris will still keep you warm even in extreme conditions. Stuff the entire shelter from top to bottom with debris. Crawl in and smash it down. Repeat stuffing and smashing until there is room for you and your debris and nothing else. It should be on the difficult side to get in, requiring much squirming for a good fit.

The last step to minimally complete your shelter is to make a door. This can be as simple as a large plug of debris pulled into the shelter after entering for milder conditions. For a better, more serviceable door, make one from woven grass or cattail leaves. Additionally, make a debris sandwich between woven sticks. In any event make sure the door is near when you squirm in so you can easily reach it when you go in.

There are two simple enhancements that will make the shelter warmer. First, build an extended igloo type entrance. Secondly, build a threshold log about three to four inches in diameter partially buried at the door. Both will provide enhanced warmth.

Make sure you do not collect poison ivy, oak, sumac, stinging nettle, buttercups or any other plant material that could inflict dermatitis or otherwise make you miserable.

The beauty of this shelter is that it will keep you warm without the hassle of tending a fire. Ensure no fires are built too close to this shelter, because the only way it could be more flammable is if you poured gas on it.

Before you crawl into your secure and warm cocoon, make sure you take care of any nature calls, as getting in and out is a little challenging. Sleep well, as you are sleeping in the womb of Mother Nature.

Scout Pit

The Scout Pit is a truly awesome shelter. This was the shelter of choice for the Apache Medicine Scout. The most famous Apache Medicine Scout, Geronimo and his small band of scouts successfully evaded capture by one third of the United States Army for over ten years. He voluntarily gave himself up several times, but he was never captured. He and his men lived in an invisible world beyond the awareness of modern man. A network of Scout Pits throughout the southwest United States played a significant role in their success.

This is an all-weather shelter that will keep you warm and dry in temperatures well below zero without the aid of fire. It will also keep you cool in desert conditions. When properly constructed it is invisible within the terrain and resistant to pedestrian or vehicular traffic. The Scout Pit will be usable with minor repairs twenty to thirty years after construction. This is the ultimate survival shelter.

To construct a Scout Pit, select a location of relative obscurity that is slightly higher than the surrounding terrain. This need only be a few inches higher to have the desired effect of channeling running rainwater around the Pit. Dig a pit six inches wider than the width of your shoulders and eighteen inches longer than your body. The depth of the Pit should be crotch deep for moderate weather use and waist deep for severe. In soft soils or sand it may be necessary to form a wall of embedded vertical sticks all the way around the interior to hold up the walls. In most soils this will not be necessary.

Before beginning, remove all debris from the area where you plan to dig and place the soil. Upon completion of the pit, make a shelf two to three inches wide around the top. The shelf should be deep enough to hold the small logs that will span the top, and one foot of debris and six inches of soil. When the entire structure is complete, it should be slightly higher than the surrounding landscape to help water runoff.

Next, construct a solid roof of sturdy sticks or split logs. Place the sticks across the width of the pit, resting on the shelf. The sticks or logs should be large enough in diameter to easily support the weight of a man without detection of sag or larger, according to your desires. The entire length of the pit is covered with logs, less an opening at the chest location just large enough to squeeze through. Place twelve inches of debris consisting of forest litter, grass or any other material that provides loft and dead air space on top of the roof. Cover the debris with six inches of soil previously removed from the pit. Cover the soil with a layer of debris. Place some small sticks on top of the debris to prevent the wind from blowing away the debris.

Disguise the Scout Pit further by transplanting local underbrush such as briers, brambles, grasses, blueberries, trees, etc. on top of the pit. Construct a tapered plug door to snugly fit into the chest door opening that is slightly larger on top than the bottom. Build the plug by making a debris sandwich from a lashed arrangement of sticks or split logs on the top and bottom. Camouflage the door appropriately. Landscape the immediate area with the remaining removed soil. Cover this soil with debris, sticks and plants as required to disguise your structure.

The last step requires completely filling the pit with debris, compressing with your body and refilling. Repeat this process until a good snug bed is created. Leave enough room to comfortably turn over while in the pit. Summer use requires less debris. When not using the Scout Pit, remove all the debris from the interior to discourage other critters from moving in.

Fish Stunners

I remember reading as a teenager about Native Americans using plant materials to stun fish in pools of water using secret plant materials. I was fascinated by this prospect, because I was always chasing after fish using various methods including a fishing pole, fish spear, archery, nets, traps, and by hand. Unfortunately I was not able to track down this allusive knowledge about this secret fish stunning plants until much later in my life. So I was temporarily denied this additional method of harvesting fish in my arsenal. Upon further research I discovered that there were many fish stunning plant sources claimed to have been used by Native Americans.

Black walnut hulls were used as a fish stunner. Enough of these crushed hulls thrown into a pool of water containing fish will stun the fish and bring them to the top for easy pickings. Yucca filamentosa leaves, stems and roots were also used as fish stunners (Meuninck, 1995). Blue Curls (Trichostema lanceolatum), Turkey mullein (Eremocarpus setigerus), Soaproot (Chlorogallum pomeridianum), and Buckeye (Aesculus spp.) were used as fish stunners (Murphey, 1990). Vinegar Weed (Trichostema spp.) and Mullein seed are as well.

In general all these plant materials are used in the same way. Bruising or shredding the materials before hand to release the essential biochemicals will enhance their efficacy. Fish stunning plant materials tend to be temporary in nature, but must be applied in sufficient quantity to have the desirable narcotic effect.

Soaps and Deodorants

Soaps

Sapponins abound in nature. Sapponins are molecular structures that attract water on one part of the molecule and oily or fatty molecules on another part. Whenever a soap product is used, one end of the saponin latches onto a water molecule and the other end latches onto fat-like molecules found in bacteria and other organic materials. When the soap is rinsed away the organic material is dragged with it.

Plants that are high in natural sapponins include Sweet Pepperbush leaves (Clethra alnifolia), and Mountain Pepperbush (Clethra acuminata). These are also known as Summer Sweet, White Alder or Soap Bush. Mountain Pepperbush is only found in the southern Appalachians.

New Jersey Tea roots (Ceanothus americanus), Bouncing Bet green plant parts (Saponaria offinales), Yucca leaves and roots (Yucca spp.), Soaproot or Soap-plant (Chlorogallum pomeridianum), and Lamb's–quarter's roots (Chenopodium album) all contain high saponin content.

Deodorants and Perfumes

Native Americans used many natural substances to hide or enhance body odor. In preparation for hunting or warfare they would begin to deodorize their body with a good sweat lodge that would flush their pores clean and purge their bodies and spirits of impurities. As part of their camouflage routine, they wanted to preclude olfactory detection as well as visual. Their main camouflaging materials consisted of charcoal and ash. Both of these materials absorb odors and give off a familiar and natural burnt wood odor. In applying some of the natural bug repellents from the mint family gave them added natural odor camouflage as well. Yarrow was commonly used as a deodorant as well. Omaha, Pawnee, and Ponca Indians used Wild Columbine (Aquilegia canadensis) seeds for perfume in courting (Coffey, 1993).

Water, Water Everywhere

Pure water is a lot more difficult to come by in nature than it was before the European conquest of America. Prior to that time the nearest stream or lake was plenty clean enough and water was plentiful. That is not the case anymore. There are still some sources of pure water directly from the earth but they are getting harder and harder to locate. It is hard to imagine that there was a day when any thirsty individual could reach down into the Ohio or Mississippi rivers and drink until satiated without fear. I would drink from my toilet before I would drink from either of these two rivers today. Although they are significantly cleaner today than twenty years ago, some people still use them as a place to put their garbage and waste. This is really a great loss for everyone.

Assume all open water is unsafe unless you have a very good reason for thinking otherwise, like having it tested. Even where there are no chemical pollutant sources, like in the middle of Alaska, there is a significant danger of contracting Giardia. Would I drink water coming from the side of mountain out of rock that I knew had nothing upstream all the way to the source? Probably yes, but how many places are there in the United States like this, not many.

Assuming there are no significant chemical pollutants to worry about, there are safe natural sources of water. Again this is a big assumption. As mentioned in the section on sugar in Culinary Substitutes, there are many tree species that can be tapped for sap. Tree sap is purified drinking water with added nutrients, including sugars. The soil and the tree's root system make great filters. Bull Thistle (Cirsium vulgare), a prickly plant with dandelion-like leaves that is commonly found in lawns and disturbed areas, is a great plant source of water. Use a knife to de-thorn the leaves and stems. It tastes like watery celery and is filled with water. Likewise Prickly Pear cactus (Opuntia humifusa) protects its precious stores of water with thorns as well.

Grapevines, particularly before the leaves have totally sprouted in spring and early summer, provide ample quantities of pure fresh drinking water. Cut the vine about four to six feet above ground level. Bend the vine down to the ground either directly into your mouth or into a water container. You will be amazed at the amount of water one vine will provide. Become familiar with Grape's poison look-alike, Canadian Moonseed (Menispermum canadense) as described in the Wet Forest Edible section. Eating the seeds of Smooth Sumac (Rhus Glabra) is said to be great thirst quencher (Duke, 1992).

Collecting morning dew with a clean towel, shirt, or sponge is a great source of pure water. Packing a clean sponge or a super absorbent cloth in your backpack is a great survival tool. If you are really in need of water and do not have anything clean, use your socks or shirt. It may taste bad, but if you are thirsty enough you probably will not care.

If you find a body of water that appears to meet the criteria for cleanliness, but you want some extra insurance, dig into the earth a foot or so away until you reach water. This water will probably be dirtier than the water on the surface due to mud, but the mud and sand will filter out most of the harmful biologicals. A simple high tech solution to filtering water may be obtained in most camping stores. There are many filter pumps available. Also check out some of the neat filter straws that allow you to drink directly from a source of water through the straw.

Bull Thistle

Toiletries

There are several natural versions of the simple luxuries of life. The dried hardened remains of Echinacea flowers were used as hair brushes by Native Americans. Once you feel one of these it becomes an obvious use. Another similar flower structure can be found from Teasel (Dispsacus sylvestris) which was also used as a carder for pulling knots out of raw wool.

Young Teasel Plants

A quick bandage for small cuts and abrasions can be made with pine pitch melted onto the wound and then dusted with wood ash. The wood ash will act as a catalyst to form an epoxy-like seal to keep the scratch clean. Toothbrushes can be made from small aromatic tree stems including Sassafras, Spicebush and Dogwood.

Toilet paper can be improvised from fresh leaves of many plants including Comfrey, Mullein, and Plantain, as well as many others. Make absolutely sure of what plant species you are grabbing, because many species such as Poison Ivy, Stinging Nettle, and Buttercups could make for a less than pleasing result. Also wet leaves from the forest floor as well as grass can also be used.

Weather Predictors

There are several weather predictors I have come to rely upon over the years that seem to be pretty accurate. Two of them are based on remembering little sayings: Red *at Night Sailors Delight; Red in Morning Sailors take Warning* and *Wind from West is Best.* The first saying concerning the red predicts for good weather the next day if the clouds are red in the evening. If the clouds are red in the morning it predicts for bad weather that day. Since most of our weather comes from the west due to the Coriolis Effect, wind from the west indicates a normal flow in the weather pattern. A sudden shift in the wind pattern, particularly from the east, may indicate the coming of a weather front. Weather fronts are usually cold or warm in nature. The cold weather front will bring on violent and relatively quick storms that usually last only for hours or perhaps days. Cold fronts are accompanied by large billowy cumulus cloud formations. Warm weather fronts on the other hand are usually not violent but may last up to several days or weeks.

Other indicators of rain include a sudden stillness in the air as well as the distinct smell of impending rain. Frogs head for high ground to avoid swift currents and birds fly lower than usual. The leaves of certain trees like maples curl upwards, exposing their silvering undersides.

Cricket Temperature

Crickets are cold-blooded insects. When the temperature increases their metabolism goes up. When the temperature goes down their metabolism also goes down. This is a generally accepted formula used to calculate cricket temperature:

$$\text{Temp (Fahrenheit)} = 39 + \text{Number of Cricket Chirps per 15 Seconds}$$

This should be remembered as a general rule. Use this rule as a basis to calibrate the particular species and gene pool of crickets in your area. To do this count the cricket chirps for 15 seconds during various temperatures. Measure the temperature with a thermometer. Calculate, average, and adjust the 39-second constant by comparing it to the measured thermometer readings. Once you have calibrated your crickets, you will have a pretty good gauge for taking the temperature throughout most of the year and a really neat way to impress your friends.

Odds and Ends

There were several neat things that did not exactly fit into any predetermined category, so I just called them odds and ends.

Cordage

There are many plants that are excellent for braiding cordage into strong strings and ropes. Some are better than others. If you are looking for really strong cordage look for one of the following plant sources. Use the inner bark unless otherwise specified:

Dogbane, also known as Indian Hemp (Apocynum spp.)
Velvetleaf, also known as Indian Mallow (Abutilon theophrasti)
Yucca (Yucca spp.) leaves
Marijuana or Hemp (Cannabis sativa) - Illegal to use or own.
Stinging Nettle (Utrica dioica)
Milkweed (Asclepias spp.)
Basswood Tree
Elm Tree

Not as good as the ones above, but still worth consideration:

Evening Primrose (Oenothera biennis)
Cattail (Typha spp.) leaves
Saw Palmetto (Serenoa repens) leaves
Cedar Tree

Aspen Tree
Willow Tree
Cottonwood Tree
Hickory Tree
Oak Tree
Ash Tree
Walnut Tree
Cherry Tree

Indiana Mallow

Pan Scrubbers, Fingernail Files, and Sandpaper

Horsetail (Equisetum spp.) feels very similar to sand paper and can be used for various functions that require an abrasive like sandpaper.

Horsetail

Torches

Cattails and Mullein seed heads attached to their long stocks and dipped in melted animal fat or hydrogenated oil make great torches that burn for a long time. Mullein is also known as the candlewick plant.

Pollution Indicators

Lichens are great indicators for air pollution. These ancient and primitive plants are very sensitive to air pollution. If the air quality is good then the Lichens will be healthy. If the air quality is poor, they will be one of the first plants to show degradation and death. Think of Lichens as the canaries of the forest.

Chapter 12: Wild Farming

"We are wont to forget that the sun looks on our cultivated fields and on the prairies and forests without distinction. They all reflect and absorb his rays alike, and the former make but a small part of the glorious picture which he beholds in his daily course. In his view the earth is all equally cultivated like a garden. Therefore we should receive the benefit of his light and beat with a corresponding trust and magnanimity."

Henry David Thoreau

Several years ago I purchased a large parcel of wooded acreage in southern Indiana. The natural biodiversity of the property was outstanding. As an added benefit, it was isolated from urban and rural pollutants due to its rural location, elevation, and adjacency to state forestry. The selective logging activity that occurred several years earlier had left the property unbalanced. The property was primarily a wet hardwood forest with a complete canopy along with a few acres of seasonal wetlands on a large creek. Very little light penetrated to the forest floor during the spring, summer and most of the fall.

There was a great abundance of woodland flora such as Bloodroot, Mayapple, Blue Cohosh, Wild Yam, and Jack-in-the-Pulpit. There were also many deciduous trees, cedars, and shrubs. Additionally the frequent presence of high order predators such as bobcat, coyote, foxes, hawks, and owls was a good indicator of the abundant fauna present.

Jack-in-the-Pulpit

I wanted to increase the biodiversity of the property by working with nature and introducing more transition areas. To accomplish this I planned to add ponds with surrounding open areas. The tree population needed to be brought into balance by culling crowded species and planting others. I wanted to achieve all of this and more without further damaging or polluting the environment.

This type of farming is known as Permaculture or Sustainable Agriculture. The main differences between Permaculture and conventional agriculture are that conventional agriculture is monoculturally based. Permaculture is polycultural based, having a great diversity of species growing together as in nature. Conventional agriculture uses fertilizer, pesticide and is energy intensive. Permaculture takes advantage of natural biosystems and biodiversity to attain similar results.

Conventional agriculture seeks maximum yields for monocultural crops. This is accomplished at the expense of the environment. It uses brute force to conquer nature removing all competition through mechanical means and herbicides and applying large quantities of petroleum based fertilizers and pesticides. This results in highly toxic nitrates and pesticides escaping into the aquifer as well as a continual loss of precious topsoil through erosion.

Permaculture on the other hand can outperform conventional agriculture when measuring total yield of multiple products per acre. Permaculture is nonpolluting and preserves and enhances topsoil and prevents erosion. This is all possible because permaculture works with nature instead of against it.

I began by constructing three one-quarter to one-half acre ponds. Two held water, one developed a cave and drained. I immediately began stocking the ponds with a self-sustaining array of flora and fauna. In both ponds I put Crayfish, Bullfrog Tadpoles, Freshwater Clams, Japanese Trapdoor Snails, Bull Minnows, Flathead Minnows, Daphnia, Jumbo Bluegill, Channel Catfish, and Largemouth Bass. Both the Clams and Snails have free-swimming offspring that would provide the food basis for the minnows. They would also filter the water as adults. The minnows, especially the bull minnows, would feed on mosquito larvae. I provided the catfish with submerged plastic garbage cans for "Brooding Caves." The bullfrogs and larger fish could feed on the crayfish. I also tossed a couple of bales of hay into the virgin ponds to give them a jump-start.

I introduced cattails by shaking cattail seed heads over the water. I also purchased watercress and transplanted Arrowhead (Sagittaria spp.). These plants would aid in providing a self-sustaining balance in the ponds and provide some great wild edibles as well. Within the first year I had volunteer great bulrush, yellow nut grass and willows establish along the pond edges. These volunteer edibles and medicinals were a welcome addition to the biodiversity.

Around the ponds I planted Grass, Mints, Korean Lezbedeza, Hairy Vetch, Day lilies, Red Clover, Purple Coneflower, Evening Primrose, Blueberries, Asparagus, Wild Strawberries, Juneberries, Nanking Cherries, and Jerusalem Artichokes.

Along the driveway I planted Grass, Red Clover, Dogbane, Day lilies, Nasturtiums, Mullein, and Burdock. In the drained pond I planted Cattails in the moist bottom and the same things I planted around the two other ponds. I also planted Blueberries, Yarrow, Coneflower, Opuntia, Gooseberries, Milkweed, and Elderberries. To complete the ponds, I erected four wood-duck nest boxes and one bat house.

Before the American Chestnut blight, one hardwood tree in four in the eastern United States was an American Chestnut. Since reintroduction of the American Chestnut would be futile due to the continued presence of the blight, I planted European-American hybrid trees. These trees will not get as big as the original American Chestnut, but will grow significantly larger than the Asian variety.

In a timbered two acres, selected for its low quality of diversity, I began by girdling the remaining trees, so they would die upright. The larger ones would provide nest sites for various animals. Beneath these trees I planted over a hundred trees including Hybrid Chestnuts, Heartnuts, Pinyon Pines, Persian Walnut, Cherry, Apple, Apricots, Ginkgo, American Persimmon Cultivars, and Monkey-Puzzle trees. The Monkey-Puzzle is a pine tree from Brazil that produces a two-inch plus pine nut. Tree protectors were placed around all these trees to ward off deer and other hungry neighbors in the forest. Underneath I planted Red Clover, Burdock, and Jerusalem Artichoke. Additionally I planted Korean Lezbedeza and Sorghum for the deer.

My future plans include planting a wild medicinal herb garden to include the following herbs, which I all ready have:

Chamomile - Digestive aid.
Echinacea - Immune enhancer.
Feverfew - Migraine relief
Pennyroyal - Bug Repellent.
Willow - Aspirin substitute.
Ginger - Soothes upset stomach, nausea relief, high blood pressure and cholesterol.
Black Cohosh - Female problems, estrogen source.
Wild Yam - Female problems.
Mullein - Constipation, congestion relief.

Yarrow - Wound Treatment, styptic, antiseptic, sedative, digestive aid.
Jewelweed - Poison Ivy and other skin rashes.
Yucca - Soap and lice treatment.
Violet - Sedative.
Wild Oats - Sedative.

I plan on adding the following:

Mountain Mint - Bug repellent.
Lemon Balm - Sedative.
Field Garlic - Everything.
Goldenseal -Antibiotic, immune enhancer.
Rosemary - Bug repellent.
Heal-all - Internal and external wound treatment, immune enhancer.
Saint John's Wort - Anti-depression and immune enhancer.
Valerian - Sedative that smells like dirty socks.

I will eventually create one or more two-acre fields to further enhance the number of transition areas. There are many other local plants that can be transplanted into the forest and in the open areas. It is not necessary to bring in animals, as the improved habit will naturally take care of that.

Eventually I may plant a small-cultivated garden of annuals. I will need to build an eight–foot fence, enhanced by electricity, to keep the wildlife on the wild side of the fence. This is the one of the few downsides in farming the wild. The wild will appreciate your enhancements as much as you do.

Almost as fast as we can destroy nature we can also preserve and enhance it. This is where we, the human animal, can fit into nature and enrich it. For further information on Permaculture see the bibliography for books by Mollison.

When you are close to nature you can listen to the voice of God.

Hermann Hesse

Bibliography

Ames, B., Magaw R., Swirsky Gold, L. 1987. <u>Ranking Possible Carcinogenic Hazards</u>, Science, Vol 236, 17 April 1987, pp 271-280

Angier, B. 1974. *Field Guide to Edible Wild Plants*. Stackpole Books, Harrisburg, PA. 254 pp.

Balch, J. F., Balch, P. A. 1990. *Prescription for Nutritional Healing*. Avery Publishing Group, Garden City Park, NY. 368 pp.

Balch, P. A., Balch, J. F. 1992. *Prescription for Cooking and Dietary Wellness*. P.A.B. Publishing, Greenfield, IN. 317 pp.

Berglund, B., Bolsby, C. 1971. *The Edible Wild*. Charles Scribner's Sons, NY. 188 pp.

Brill, S., Dean, E. 1994. *Identifying and Harvesting Edible and Medicinal Plants*. Hearst Books, NY pp. 317

Britton, N.L., Brown, A. 1970. *An Illustrated Flora of the Northern United States and Canada*. Dover Publications Inc., NY. Three volumes.

Brown, L. 1979. *Grasses: An Identification Guide*. Houghton Mifflin. NY. 240 pp.

Brown, T. 1985. *Tom Brown's Guide to Wild Edible and Medicinal Plants*. Berkley Books, NY, NY. 241 pp.

Buchman, D. D. 1979. *Herbal Medicine - The Natural Way to Get Well and Stay Well*. Gramercy Publishing Company, NY, NY. 310 pp.

Carper, J. 1993. *Food- Your Miracle Medicine*. Harper Collins, NY. 528 pp.

Carper, J. 1997. *Miracle Cures*. Harper Collins, NY. 308 pp.

Castleman, M. 1991. *The Healing Herbs*. Rodale Press, Emmaus, PA. 436 pp.

Castleman, M. 1995. <u>Recent Findings in Healing Herbs</u>, The Herb Quarterly, Fall 1995. Pp 38-41.

Coffey, T. 1993. *The History and Folklore of North American Wildflowers,* Facts on File, Inc. NY. 356 pp.

CF - Coltsfoot; In Appreciation of Wild Plants; (Six Issues a Year (Volume 15 in 1994)). Last year published 1994. Back issues available for $10.00 from: Jim Troy, Box 313A, Shipman, VA 22971

Deam, C. C. 1940, *Flora of Indiana* . Department of Conservation, Division of Forestry, Indianapolis, IN. 1236 pp.

Deam, C. C. 1953, *Trees of Indiana* . Historic Hoosier Hills Woodland Committee, Versailles, IN. 330 pp.

Deam, C. C. 1995, *Shrubs of Indiana* . Historic Hoosier Hills Woodland Committee, Versailles, IN. 380 pp.

Duke, J. A. 1986. *Handbook of Northeastern Indian Medicinal Plants.* Quarterman Publications, Lincoln, MA. 212 pp.

Duke, J. A. 1992. *Handbook of Edible Weeds.* CRC Press, Boca Raton, FL. 246 pp.

Duke, J. A. 1997. *The Green Pharmacy.* Rodale Press, Emmaus, PA. 507 pp.

Elias, T. S., Dykeman, P. A. 1982. *Field Guide to North American Edible Wild Plants.* Outdoor Life Books, NY. 286 pp.

Elliot, D. 1995. *Wild Roots: A Forager's Guide to the Edible and Medicinal Roots, Tubers, Corms, and Rhizomes of North America.* Healing Arts Press, Wochester, Vermont. 128 pp.

Facciola, S. 1990. *Cornucopia - A Sourcebook of Edible Plants.* Kampong Publications, Vista, CA 678 pp.

Fernald, M. L. 1950. *Grays Manual of Botany* Eighth (Centennial Edition) - Illustrated. Dioscorides Press, Portland, Oregon. 1632 pp.

Fernald M.L. and Kinsey C.A. 1958. *Edible Wild Plants of Eastern North America.* Dover Publications, NY. 452 pp.

Foster, S., Duke, J. A. 1990. *Peterson Field Guide to Medicinal Plants.* Houghton Mifflin Company, Boston MA. 366 pp.

Foster, S. 1991. *Echinacea- Nature's Immune Enhancer.* Healing Arts Press, Rochester, NY. 150 pp.

Foster, S., Caras, R. 1994. *Venomous Animals & Poisonous Plants.* Peterson Filed Guides. Houghton Mifflin Company, Boston MA. 244 pp.

Foster, S. 1995. *Forest Pharmacy.* Forest History Society, Durham, NC. 57 pp.

Gail, P. 1989. *The Delightful Delicious Daylily.* Goosefoot Acres Press, Cleveland, Ohio. 66 pp.

Gail, P. 1994. *The Dandelion Celebration.* Goosefoot Acres Press, Cleveland, Ohio. 156 pp.

Gail, P. 1994. *Violets in the Kitchen.* Goosefoot Acres Press, Cleveland, Ohio. 58 pp.

Gibbons, E. 1962. *Stalking the Wild Asparagus.* Alan C. Hood and Company, Putney, Vermont. 303 pp.

Gibbons, E. 1971. *Stalking the Good Life*. David Mckay Company, NY. 247 pp.

Gleason, H., Cronquist, A. 1991. *Manual of Vascular Plants of Northeastern United States and Adjacent Canada*. The New York Botanical Garden, Bronx, NY. 910 pp.

Grainger, J., Moore, C. 1991. *Natural Insect Repellents for Pets, People and Plants*. The Herb Bar, Austin, TX. 152 pp.

Grieve, M. 1981. *A Modern Herbal*. [Reprint] Dover publications, NY, NY. 902 pp.

Hamel P. B., Chiltoskey, M.U. 1975. *Cherokee Plants: their uses* - A 400 Year History. Paul B. Hamel and Mary Chiltoskey. 72 pp.

Harris, B. 1971. *Eat The Weeds*. Barre Publishers, Garre, MA. 223 pp.

Hedrick, U.P. 1972. *Sturtvant's Edible Plants of the World*. Dover Publications, NY. 686 pp.

Heinerman, J. 1988. *Heinerman's Encyclopedia of Fruits, Vegetables and Herbs,* Parker Publishing Co. West Nyack, NY. 400 pp.

Hill, S. 1985. *100 Poisonous Plants of Maryland.* The University of Maryland Cooperative Extension Service. 55 pp.

Hitchcock, A. S. *Manual of Grasses of the United States.* Second Edition, Volumes one and two, Dover, NY. 1051 pp.

Hobbs, C. 1994. *Ginkgo- Elixir of Youth*. Botanica Press, Capitola, CA. 80 pp.

Hoffman, D. L. 1994. *The Herbalist.* [CD-ROM Macintosh Ver 2.0M]. Hopkins Technology, Hopkins, MN.

Hunt, D. 1992. *Native Indian Wild game Fish and Wild Foods Cookbook.* Fox Chapel Publishing, Lancaster, PA. 281 pp.

Hyatt, R. 1978. *Chinese Herbal Medicine - Ancient Art and Modern Science*. Schocken Books, NY, NY. 160 pp.

James, W. R. 1973. *Know Your Poisonous Plants*. Naturegraph Publishers, Inc., Happy Camp, CA. 99 pp.

Kowalchik, C., Hylton, W. 1987. *Illustrated Encyclopedia of Herbs*. Rodale Press, Emmaus PA. 545 pp.

MacNicol, M. 1967. *Flower Cookery: The Art of Cooking with Flowers*. Fleet Press Corporation, NY. 263 pp.

Mann, R. 1991. *Backyard Sugarin'*. The Countryman Press, Woodstock, VT. 95 pp.

Martin, C. 1991. *Earthmagic - Finding and Using Medicinal Herbs.* The Countryman Press, Woodstock, VT. 228 pp.

McPherson, A., McPherson, S. 1977. *Wild Edible Plants of Indiana.* Indiana University Press, Bloomington, IN. 215 pp.

Meyer, J. E. 1976. *The Herbalist.* [Reprint] Meyerbooks, Glenwood, IL. 304 pp.

Meuninck, J. and Duke, J. A. 1988. *Edible Wild Plants - Video Field Guide to 100 Useful Herbs.* Media Methods, Edwardsburg, MI. 60 min video.

Meuninck, J. and Duke, J. A. 1990. *Trees Shrubs Nuts and Berries - Video Cookbook and Field Guide.* Media Methods, Edwardsburg, MI. 60 min video.

Meuninck, J. and Duke, J. A. 1992. *Natural Healing with Medicinal Herbs and Healing Foods.* Media Methods, Edwardsburg, MI. 60 min.

Meuninck, J. 1995. *Little Medicine: the Wisdom to Avoid Big Medicine.* Media Methods, Edwardsburg, MI. 60 min.

Millspaugh, C.F. 1974. *American Medicinal Plants.* Dover Publications, NY. 806 pp.

Mollison B., Holmgren, D. 1987. *Permaculture One.* Tagari Publications, Tyalgum, NSW 2484, Australia. 127 pp.

Mollison B. 1987. *Permaculture Two.* Tagari Publications, Tyalgum, NSW 2484, Australia. 150 pp.

Moulton, L. 1993. *The Herb Walk* [Video]. L. M. Publications, Provo, Utah. 75 min.

Moulton, L. 1993. *The Herb Walk Manual.* L. M. Publications, Provo, Utah. 94 pp.

Moulton, L. 1977. *Natures Medicine Chest.* Herb identification cards. L. M. Publications, Provo, Utah. 94 pp.

Mowrey, D. E. 1986 *The Scientific Validation of Herbal Medicine.* Keats Publishing, New Canaan, CN. 316 pp.

Murphey, E. V. A. 1990. *Indian Uses of Native Plants.* Meyerbooks, Glenwood, Illinois. 81 pp.

Newcomb, L. 1977. *Newwcomb's Wildflower Guide.* Little, Brown and Company, Boston, MA. 490 pp.

Niethammer, C. 1974. *American Indian Food and Lore.* Collier Books, NY 191 pp.

Novick, N. 1994. *You can do Something About Your Allergies.* MacMillan Publishing, NY. 211 pp.

Nyerges, C. 1997. *Better Health from Common Plants*. Backwoods Home Magazine. Jan/Feb 1997. pp 35-37.

Ocean, S. 1993, *Acorns and Eat'em*, Ocean-Hose, Willitis, CA. 86 pp.

Persons, W. S. 1994. *American Ginseng - Green Gold*. Bright Mountain Books, Ashville, NC. 201 pp.

Peterson, L. 1978. *Peterson Field Guides - A Field Guide to Wild Edible Plants*. Houghton Mifflin, Boston MA. 330 pp.

Philip, S., Philip, F., Meuninck, J. 1990. *Cooking with Edible Flowers*. Media Methods, Edwardsburg, MI. 60 min video.

Quillin, P. 1994. *The Wisdom of Amish Folk Medicine*. The Leader Company, North Canton, OH. 58 pp.

Reader's Digest, 1986. *Magic and Medicine of Plants*. Reader's Digest, Pleasantville, NY. 464 pp.

Symonds, G.W.D. 1958. *The Tree Identification Book*. Quill, NY . 272 pp.

Symonds, G.W.D. 1963. *The Shrub Identification Book*. William Morrow and Company, NY . 379 pp.

Squire, T.K. 1996. *The Wild and Free Cookbook*. Loompanics Unlimited, Port Townsend, Washington. 295 pp.

Squire, T.K. 1989. *Living Off the Land*. Academy Books, Rutland, VT. 133 pp.

Schar, D. 1993. *Thirty Plants That Could Save Your Life*. Elliot and Clark Publishing, Wash, DC. 134 pp.

Stuart, M. 1979. *The Encyclopedia of Herbs and Herbalism*. First Grosset and Dunlap, NY. 304 pp.

Tatum, B.J. 1976. *Billy Joe Tatum's Wild Foods Cookbook and Field Guide*. Workman Publishing Company, NY 268 pp.

Trelease, W. 1967. *Winter Botany: An identification guide to native trees and shrubs*. Dover Publications, Inc. NY, NY. 396 pp.

Tyler, V. 1985. *Hoosier Home Remedies.*. Purdue University Press, West Lafayette, IN. 212 pp.

Tyler, V. 1994. *Herbs of Choice: The Therapeutic Use of Phytochemicals*. Pharmaceutical Products Press, NY. 209 pp.

Tyler, V. 1993. *The Honest Herbal: A Sensible Guide to The Use of Herbs and Related Remedies.* Third edition. Pharmaceutical Products Press, NY. 375 pp.

University Medical Research Publishers. 1993. *Amazing Medicines the Drug Companies Don't Want You To Discover!.* University Medical Research Publishers, Tempe, AZ. 379 pp.

Vogel, V. J. 1977. *American Indian Medicine.* University of Oklahoma Press. 585 pp.

Weil, A., 1995. *Spontaneous Healing.* Fawcett Columbine, NY pg 254.

Weiner, M.A. 1972. *Earth Medicine-Earth Foods.* Collier Books, NY. 214 pp.

WFF - Wild Foods Forum; (Six Issues a Year (Volume 7 in 1996)). Available for $15.00 from: The Wild Foods Forum, PO Box 61413, Virginia Beach, VA 23466-1413

Wren, R.W. 1972. *Potter's New Cyclopaedia of Medical Herbs and Preparations.* Harper Colophon Books, NY. 400 pp.

Appendix A: Favorite References

I am often asked to name my favorite references from the myriads of those available. Below I have listed some of my favorites.

Identification Books

Identifying and Harvesting Edible and Medicinal Plants. By Brill and Dean.

Peterson Field Guides - A Field Guide to Wild Edible Plants. By Peterson.

Peterson Field Guide to Medicinal Plants. By Foster and Duke.

Newcomb's Wildflower Guide by Newcomb.

Field Guide to North American Edible Wild Plants by Elias and Dykeman.

The Illustrated Book of Wildflowers and Shrubs by Grimm.

Venomous Animals & Poisonous Plants. by Caras.

More Technical References

Grays Manual of Botany Eighth (Centennial Edition) - Illustrated by Fernald.

Manual of Vascular Plants of Northeastern United States and Adjacent Canada by Gleason and Cronquist.

Flora of Indiana by Charles Deam.

An Illustrated Flora of the Northern United States and Canada. By Britton and Brown in three volumes.

Cookbooks

The Dandelion Celebration by Peter Gail
Violets in the Kitchen. by Peter Gail
The Delightful Delicious Daylily by Peter Gail
Persimmon Recipes by Dymple Green
Stalking the Wild Asparagus by Euell Gibbons
Stalking the Good Life by Euell Gibbons
Billy Joe Tatum's Wild Foods Cookbook and Field Guide. by Billy Joe
Flower Cookery: The Art of Cooking with Flowers by Mary MacNicol
The Wild and Free Cookbook by Tom Squire
Living Off the Land by Tom Squire

Native American Plant Use Books

Duke, J. A. 1986. *Handbook of Northeastern Indian Medicinal Plants*. Quarterman Publications, Lincoln, MA. 212 pp.

Murphey, E. V. A. 1990. *Indian Uses of Native Plants*. Meyerbooks, Glenwood, Illinois. 81 pp.

Other Plant Use Books

Creasy, Rosalind, 1982. *The Complete Book of Edible Landscaping*, Sierra Club Books, San Francisco. 379 pp.

Facciola, S. 1990. *Cornucopia - A Sourcebook of Edible Plants*. Kampong Publications, Vista, CA 678 pp.

Kourik, Robert, 1986. *Designing and Maintaining Your Edible Landscape Naturally*. Metamorphic Pres, Santa Rosa, CA. 370 pp.

Herb and Natural Healing Books

Carper, J. 1993. *Food- Your Miracle Medicine*. Harper Collins, NY. 528 pp.

Carper, J. 1997. *Miracle Cures*. Harper Collins, NY. 308 pp.

Castleman, M. 1991. *The Healing Herbs*. Rodale Press, Emmanaus, PA. 436 pp.

Duke, J. A. 1997. *The Green Pharmacy*. Rodale Press, Emmaus, PA. 507 pp.

Kowalchik, C., Hylton, W. 1987. *Illustrated Encyclopedia of Herbs*. Rodale Press, Emmaus PA. 545 pp.

Newsletters

Coltsfoot
No longer currently published back issues available for $2 per issue or $10 for a year set of six. Write to:

Jim Troy
Box 313A
Shipman, VA 22971

The Food Insect Newsletter
Department of Entomology
324 Leon Johnson Hall
Montana State University

Bozeman, MT 59717-0302
($5.00 for one year subscription)

The Forager
Box 692110
Houston, TX 77269-2110

($15.00 for one year subscription)

The Wild Foods Forum
P.O. Box 61413
Virginia Beach, VA 23462
(Annual Subscription: $15.00 for 6 issues)

Magazines

Earthworks Magazine
PO. Box 20
Victor, Idaho 83455
(1 year 6 issues for $14)

Backwoodsman Magazine
PO Box 627
Westcliffe, CO 81252
(1 year 6 issues for $16)

Wilderness Way Magazine
PO Box 203
Lufkin, TX 75902-0203
(1 year 4 issues for $16)

Web Pages of Interest

The Crayfish Home Page
http://www.utexas.edu/depts/tnhc/.www/crayfish/crayhome.html

Insect Recipes
http://www.ent.iastate.edu/Misc/InsectsAsFood.html

NewCROP HomePage
http://www.hort.purdue.edu/newcrop/home

Plant Tracker
http://www.axis-net.com/pfaf/
http://www.axis-net.com/pfaf/plants.html

Dining on the Wild
http://www.eee.org/bus/nature/home.html

WEEDFEED - The Useful Wild Plants of Texas
http://www.emultimedia.com/weedfeed/

Internet Directory for Botany: Economic Botany, Ethnobotany
http://fadr.msu.ru/~herba/mirrors/kmus/botecon.html

Plant Choices - Phytochemeco Databases
http://www.ars-grin.gov/~ngrlsb/plants.html

Farmacy query
http://sun.ars-grin.gov/~ngrlsb/farmacy.html

The Ethnobotany cafe on the Web
http://countrylife.net/ethnobotany/

HerbNET - University
http://www.herbnet.com/university.html

Plants for a future
http://www.liv.ac.uk/~rmorris/pfaf/

American Indian Ethnobotany Database
http://www.umd.umich.edu/cgi-bin/herb

Herbal Hall
http://www.crl.com/~robbee/herbal.html

Alternative Medicine Homepage
http://www.pitt.edu/~cbw/altm.html

Herb FAQ
http://frank.mtsu.edu/~sward/herb/herb-faq.html

Wilderness School Home Page
http://www.ccs.neu.edu/home/jstevens/wild/schools/schools.html

Horizon Herbs
http://www.chatlink.com/~herbseed/Welcome.htm

Appendix B: Where to Buy

Herb Seed and Plant Sources

Companion Plants
7247 North Ridge Road
Athens, Ohio 45701
(614) 592-4643

Well-Sweep Herb Farm
317 Mt. Bethel Road
Port Murray, New Jersey 07865
(908) 852-5390

Horizon Herbs
PO Box 69
Williams, OR 97544-0069
(541) 846-6704

Cookbooks and Foods

Dymple's Delight
Route 4, Box 53
Mitchell, IN 47446
(Persimmon Pulp and Cookbooks)

Goosefoot Acres Press
P.O. Box 18016
Cleveland, OH 44118-0016
(216) 932-2145

(Dandelion, Violets, and Day Lily cookbooks, Dandelion Coffee)

Nutcrackers and Sugarin Supplies etc.

Lehmans
One Lehman Circle
P.O. Box 41
Kidron, OH 44636
(216) 857-5757
e-mail: GetLehmans@aol.com
http://www.lehmans.com

Cumberland General Store
Route 3
Crossville, TN 38555

(800) 334-4640
(800) 484-8481

G.H. Grimm Company
P.O. Box 130
Rutland, VT 05702
(802) 775-5411

Leader Evaporator Co., Inc.
25 Stowell Street
St Albans, VT 05478
(802) 524-3931
(802) 524-4966

Nature Books and Educational Resources

Acorn Naturalist
17300 East 17th Street
#J-236
Tustin, CA 92780
(800) 422-8886
http://www.acorn-group.com

Conservation Biology Books
Patricia Ledlie Bookseller, Inc.
One Bean Road
P.O. Box 90
Buckfield, ME 04220
(207) 336-2778
email: ledlie@maine.com
http://www.booknotes.com/ledlie/

Used Edible Plant and Herb Books

O.T.B.H.
P.O. Box 11337
Minneapolis, MN, 55411
(write for latest listing)

Tree Sources

Abundant Life Seed Foundation
P.O. Box 772
Port Townsend, WA 98368

Bigelow Nurseries
P.O. Box 718
Northboro, MA 01532
(508) 845-2143
(Spicebush)

Bear Creek Nursery
P.O. Box 411
Northport, WA 99157
(Pawpaws and Persimmons)

Buddies Nursery
P.O. Box 14
Birdsboro, PA 19508
(215) 582-2410
(Spicebush)

**Burnt Ridge Nursery
and Orchards**
432 Burnt Ridge Road
Onalaska, WA 98570
206) 985-2873

Corwin Davis Nursery
RFD 1, 20865 Junction Road
Bellevue, MI 49021
(Pawpaws)

Dymple's Delight
Route 4, Box 53
Mitchell, IN 47446
812-849-3487
(Canned Persimmon Pulp,
Select Seeds, Persimmon Recipes)

Edible Landscape
RT 2, Box 77
Afton, VA 22920
800-524 4156
804-361-913
(Persimmons, Pawpaws, etc.)

Gurney's
110 Capital Street
Yankton, South Dakota 57079
(605) 665-1930

Miller Nurseries Inc.
5060 West Lake Road
Canandaigua, NY 14424
(800) 828-9630
(Persimmons)

Nichols Garden Nursery
1190 North Pacific Highway
Albany, OR 97321-4598
(541) 928-9280

Northwoods Nursery
28696 S. Cramer Road
Molalla, OR 97038
(503) 651-3737
(Persimmons)

Oikos Tree Crops
P.O. Box 19425
Kalmazoo, MI 49019
(616) 342-6504

Raintree Nursery
391 Butts Road
Morton, WA 98356

Sheffield's Seed Co.
273 Auburn Road
Route 34
Locke, NY 13092
(315) 497-1058
(Spicebush)

Warren County Nursery, Inc.
Rt 2, Box 204
McMinnville, TN 37110
(615) 668-8941
(Spicebush)

Mushroom Spore

Mushroompeople
P.O. Box 159
11435 State Rt. 1
Inverness, CA 94937
(615) 964-2200

Fungi Perfecti.
P.O. Box 7634
Olympia, WA 98507
(206) 426-9292

Fish, Tadpoles, Shellfish and Aquatic Plants

Zetts Tri State Fish Farm and Hatchery
Rt 2 Box 218K
Inwood, WV 25428
(304) 229-3654

Van Winkles Fish Hatchery
507 State Road 145
Birdseye, IN 47513
(812) 338-3499

Appendix C: Schools

Alabama

Children of the Earth
105 Orange Ave.
Fairhope, AL 36532
(334) 928-0436
http://ns1.maf.mobile.al.us/users/children/

Arizona

Anasazi
P.O. Box 795
Payson, AZ 85547

California

Earth Skills
1113 Cougar Ct, HC2 Box 8132
Frazier Park, CA 93225
(805) 245-0318

Headwaters Outdoor School
P.O. Box 1698
Santa Cruz, CA 95061-1690
(408) 423-3830

Miwok Archeological Preserve of Marin
2255 Las Gallinas
San Rafael, CA 94903

Sasquatch Way
Nachshon Rose
P.O. Box 2143
Simi Valley, CA 93062
(805) 522-7344

Wild Foods Co, Inc.
13239 W. Shadow hills Drive
Sun City West, AZ 35375
(602) 933-8675

Idaho

Boulder Outdoor Survival School
PO Box 905
Rexburg, ID, 83440
(208) 359-2400

Indiana

Bittersweet Cultural Center
8642 W. 400 N.
Rochester, IN 46975
(219) 542-2506

Wilderness Survival and Tracking
S. Claire Whalen, OSF, Michaela Farm
P.O. Box 100
Oldenburg, IN 47036

Maine

Mike and Karen's Good Earth School
RFD 1 Box 1041
Augusta, ME 04330
(207) 623-7298

Maryland

John Fishback, Natural Resouce Ecologist
John Fishback
2491 Davidsonville Rd.
Gambrills, MD 21054
(410) 451-1434

Massachusetts

Paul Rezendes Tracking School
Bearsden Road Star Route
South Royalston, MA 01331
(508) 249-8810

Montana

Earth-Heart
P.O. Box 1146
Livingston, MT 59047
(406)222-9840

New Jersey

The Tracker, Inc.
P.O. Box 173
Asbury, NJ 08802-0173
(908) 479-4681

New Mexico

The Tracking Project
PO Box 266
Corales, NM 87048

New York

Hawk Circle Wilderness Summer Camps
Hawk Circle Programs
55 Hickory Road, Apt #3
Ghent, NY 12075
(518) 672-6337

Ancient Skills School
c/o Joe Longshore II
357 Cowan Rd.
Canton, NY 13617

Deep Wilds
18 Austain Ave.
Albany, NY 12205
(518) 438-0923
deepwilds@aol.com

Northeast School of Botanical Medicine
PO Box 6626
Ithaca, NY 14851
(607) 564-1023

Rune Hill Retreat and Awareness Center
Box 413
Spencer, NY 14883

Wilderness Way - Primitive Skills, Tracking, Nature Awareness School
744 Glenmary Drive
Owego, NY 13827
(607) 687-9186

Oregon

Coyotes Path
P.O. Box 18145
Portland, OR 97218
(503) 284-3076

Virginia

Nature Awareness School
P.O. Box 210
Lyndhurst, VA 22950
(703) 377-6068

Nature's Nurture
2305 Park Avenue
Richmond, VA 23220
(804) 358-4060
(Wild Edibles courses)

Washington

EarthWalk Northwest, Inc.
PO Box 461
Issaquah, WA 98027
(Conducts courses on east coast as well)
(206) 746-7267

Wilderness Awareness Schools
16625 Redmond Way, Suite M 447
Redmond, WA 98052
(800) 340-6068, (206) 702-0622 (in WA)

North Cascades Institute
2105 S.R. 20
Sedro-Woolley, WA 98284-9394

The Whidbey Institute
PO Box 57
Clinton, WA 98236

<u>Wisconson</u>

Northern Quest Learning Center
7273 Chicken-in-the-Woods Rd.
Three Lakes, WI 54562
(715) 546-2329

Medicine Hawk Wilderness Skills, Inc.
P.O. Box 07482
Milwaukee, WI 53207
(414) 482-8722

Teaching Drum Outdoor School
7124 Military Rd.
Three Lakes, WI 54562

Appendix D: Videos

L. M. Publications
P.O. Box 482
Provo, Utah 84603
(801) 374-1858
(LeArta Moulton does a great job on her Herb Walk video)

Media Methods
24097 North Shore Drive
Edwardsburg, MI 49112
(Several great edible and medicinal plant videos)

Desert Vista Productions
5309 N. 28th Drive
Phoenix, AZ 85017

Backwoods Survival Skills
P.O. Box 2303
Lenoir, NC 28645

Prarie Wolf
PO Box 96
Randolf, KS 66554

General Index

A

abrasions, 104, 138
Abutilon theophrasti, 139
Acer spp., 90
Achillea millefolium, 102
acoric acid, 122
acorns, 7, 8, 53, 89
Acorus calamus, 15, 31, 84, 119
Adventure Trail, 37
Aesculus spp., 135
Aethusa cynapium, 81
African Violets, 42
Allantoin, 103
Allaria esculenta, 25, 40, 85
All-heal, 120
Allium canadense, 79, 114, 121
Allium cernuum, 62
Allium tricoccum, 47
Allium vineale, 79, 109, 110, 114, 121
Allspice, 86
Aloe vera, 104, 116
Along, 2, 90, 145
Amaranth, xvii, xviii, 65, 72, 119
Amaranthus, xviii, 72
Amaranthus spp., 72
American Chestnut, 109, 145
American Chestnut blight, 145
American Ephedra, 106
American Ginseng, 120, 151
American Holly, 86
American Linden Tree, 119
American Lotus, 31, 92
American Mountain Ash, 89
American Persimmon, 57, 58, 60, 145
American Persimmon Tree, 57
Angelic, 51
Angelic atropurpurea, 51
Anti-depression, 146
antimicrobial, 102
antiseptic, 16, 102, 114, 116, 146
Apios americana, 29, 37
Apocynum spp., 139
apple, 1, 55
Apricots, 145
Aquilegia canadensis, 135
Aralia, 50, 51
Aralia genus, 51
Aralia hispida, 51
Aralia nudicaulis, 51
Aralia racemosa, 51
Aralia spinosa, 50
Arctium spp., 72, 102
Arisaema atrorubens, 32
Arisaema triphyllum, 37
Armoracea lapathifolia, 85
Arrow Arum, 32, 92
Arrowhead, 31, 32, 92, 145

Asarum canadense, 43, 84, 113, 114, 117
Asclepias spp., 139
Asclepias syriaca, 112
ash, 16, 73, 102, 128, 129, 135, 138
Asian Ginger, 117
Asimina parviflora, 54
Asimina triloba, 54, 110
Asparagus, 145
Aspen, 127, 140
aspirin, 30, 101, 102
astringent, 8
Atamasco-lily, 69
Avena sativa, 118

B

bandage, 138
Barbarea verna, 90
Barbarea vulgaris, 25, 90
basketry, 128
bass, 95
Basswood, 119, 127, 139
Bear Grass, 71
bears, 39, 123
Bedstraw, 76
Bee Balm, 78, 110, 119
Beech, 53, 127
bees, 74, 108
bergamot, 78
Betula alba, 89
Betula lenta, 89, 101
Betula lutea, 89
Betula nigra, 89
Betula spp., 90
Birch, 89, 90, 102, 127, 128
Black Cohosh, 37, 109, 145
Black Locust, 47
Black Mustard, 25
Black Raspberries, 29
Black Snakeroot, 109
Black Walnut, 53, 110, 121
Black Willow, 101
Blackberries, 26, 53
Blackberry, 2, 26, 29, 77, 115
Bloodroot, 122, 143
blowing straws, 12
Blue Curls, 135
Blue Flag, 15, 31, 47
Blue Lettuces, 76
Blueberries, 7, 9, 26, 27, 29, 114, 145
Boehmaria cylindrica, 43
Bouncing Bet, 135
bow drill, 125
Box Elder, 127
Bracken, 41
Brambles, 7, 26, 53, 65

Brasenia schreberi, 31
Brassica nigra, 25
Brassica rapa, 25
Briers, 40, 75, 128
Bristly Sarsaparilla, 51
Broccoli Theory, 3
Bromus cathaticus, 11
Brooding Caves, 145
bruises, 16, 22
Buckeye, 135
Bug Repellent, 145
Bull Minnows, 145
Bull Thistle, 2, 136
Bullbriers, 40
bullfrogs, 93, 145
Bullhead-Lily, 31
bur oaks, 7
Burdock, 2, 72, 102, 111, 145
burns, 8, 16, 22, 104
Butternut, 53

C

cactus, 21, 22, 136
caffeine, 76, 106, 121
Calamus, 122
California, 7, 8, 163
Camas, 47, 80
Canada, 1, 20, 75, 86, 101, 147, 149, 153
Canada Thistle, 86
Canadian Moonseed, 39, 136
cancer, xviii, 41, 119, 120
Cannabis sativa, 139
canola oil, 25
Capsella bursa-pastoris, 73
carcinogenic, 37, 113
carcinogens, xv, xvii, 37
Cardamine bulbosa, 47, 85
carrot, 31, 72, 80, 81
Carya illinoensis, 54
Carya spp., 53, 90
Catbrier, 40
catfish, 95, 97, 145
Catnip, 2
cattail, 15, 16, 33, 122, 133, 145
Ceanothus americanus, 135
Cedar, 127, 139
Cercis canadensis, 46
chamomile, 104, 114
Channel Catfish, 145
chemosterilant, 122
Chenopodium album, xviii, 2, 22, 119, 121, 135
Chenopodium quinoa, 23
Cherokee, 54, 87, 104, 116, 149
Cherry, 89, 101, 102, 127, 140, 145
Cherry Birch, 89, 101, 102
Chestnuts, 145
Chickweed, 2, 65, 68, 71
Chicory, 76
chiggers, 27

chinese, 91
Chlorogallum pomeridianum, 135
cholesterol, 68, 119, 145
Chrysanthemum cinraiifolium, 122
Chrysanthemum parthenium, 104, 119, 122
Chufa, 29
Cichorium intybus, 76
Cicuta maculata, 31, 81, 85
Cimicifuga racemosa, 37, 109
Cirsium arvense, 86
Cirsium vulgare, 136
Citronelle, 122
clams, 98
Claviceps purpurea, 12
Claytonia spp., 40, 68
Clearweed, 43
Cleavers, 44, 76
Clethra acuminata, 135
Clethra alnifolia, 135
Clover, 65
Cockleburs, 72
Cold, 111, 132, 138
Collinsonia canadensis, 122
Coltsfoot, 110, 113, 147, 154
Columbine, 135, 152
Comfrey, 103, 138
communal living, 131
Coneflower, 145
congestion, 145
Conium macullatum, 31
Constipation, 115, 145
Cordage, 139
Coriolis, 138
Cornus florida, 86
Cossack Asparagus, 15, 16
Cottonwood, 127, 140
Crab Apples, 2
Cranberries, 29
crawdads, 98
crayfish, 97, 98, 99, 145, 155
Crested Dwarf Iris, 47
Cricket, 139
cruciferae, 25
crucifix vegetables, 25
cultivars, 1, 10, 55, 72, 118
Curled Dock, 24
Custard Apple, 54
cuts, 8, 16, 22, 62, 104, 138
Cyperus esculentus, 29

D

Daffodils,, 69
Dandelion, xvii, 3, 7, 20, 65, 76, 77, 90, 104, 118, 119, 121, 127, 148, 153, 157
Daphnia, 145
Darnel, 11
Datura Stramonium, 109
Daucus carota, 31, 80
Day-lilies, 15, 65, 69, 91

Debris Hut, 131, 132, 133
deer, 7, 11, 27, 89, 123, 145
delirium, 12
Delphiniums, 122
demonic possession, 12
Dentaria laciniata, 73
Dentaria spp., 40, 85
deodorant, 135
Depression, 117
dermatitis, 50, 133
Dewberries, 26, 53
diarrhea, 69, 115
digestive aid., 146
Digitalis spp., 101
Diospyros texana, 57
Diospyros virginiana, 57, 104
Diospyros virginiana var pubescens, 57
Dispsacus sylvestris, 137
Dock, 72
Dogbane, 127, 139, 145
drinking straws, 12
duck potato, 32
Duck Potatoes, 92
Duckweed, 34
Dwarf Pawpaw, 54

E

Earl Gray Tea, 78
Early Wintercress, 90
Earth Apple, 91
Echinacea, 105, 109, 117, 120, 137, 145, 148
Echinacea pallida, 117
Echinacea purpurea, 109
Echinacea spp., 105, 120
egg shell, 128
Elder, 65, 67, 127, 129
Elderberries, 145
Elderberry, 67, 74, 110, 113, 117
Eleuterococus senticosus, 120
Elm, 127, 139
Ephedra nevadensis, 106, 117
Ephedra sinica, 106
Ephedraceae, 106
ephedrine, 106, 117
epoxy, 128
Equisetum spp., 106, 141
Eremocarpus setigerus, 135
Ergot, 12
Ergotamine, 12
Ergotism, 12
Ergotoxine, 12
estrogen, 145
Euell Gibbons, xvii, 9, 15, 25, 42, 54, 65, 66, 91, 153
European, 3, 20, 25, 72, 92, 117, 120, 135
Evening Primrose, 73, 85, 123, 139, 145

F

Fagas grandifolia, 53

False Solomon-Seal, 43
False-nettle, 43
Female problems, 145
Fetid Shrub, 54
Feverbush, 86
Feverfew, 104, 119, 122, 145
Field Garlic, 79, 110, 114, 117, 119, 121, 146
Field Mustard, 25
Field Onion, 2
Filtering, 128
Fingernail Files, 141
Fireweed, 127
Firewood ash, 129
Firs, 10, 127
Fish, 92, 134, 135, 149, 161
Fish Stunners, 134
Flathead Minnows, 145
Florida, 21, 40, 54, 57, 97
Flowering Dogwood, 86
Flu, 117
Foxglove, 101, 103
freshwater clam, 98, 129
Freshwater Clams, 145
Frogs, 92, 93, 94, 139
fungicide, 110
fungus, 12, 122

G

Galium aparine, 44
Galium spp., 76
Galium verum, 86
Garlic, 2, 25, 40, 79, 85, 92, 114, 117, 119
Garlic Mustard, 25, 40, 85, 92
Gaultheria procumbens, 101
Gaylussacia spp., 27
Gelatin, 84
giardia, 115
Giardia lamblia, 115
Ginger, 84, 117, 120, 145
Ginkgo, xviii, 117, 145, 149
Ginkgo biloba, xviii, 117
Ginseng, 51, 62, 111, 120
Gleditsia triacanthos, 47
Gleditsia trianthos, 76
gluten, 16, 92
Gobo, 72
Goldenrod, 77
Goldenseal, 62, 111, 116, 120, 122, 146
Gooseberries, 145
Goosefoot, 22, 69, 148, 157
Goosegrass, 44, 76
Grape seed extract, 120
Grapes, 39, 89
grasshoppers, 100
Great Bulrush, 33
Green Frog, 94
Greenbrier, 40, 84
Ground Ivy, 2
groundhog, 87

173

Groundnut, 29, 37
grubs, 100
Gumbo Filé, 37
Gymnocladus dioica, 47
Gymnoclaudus dioica, 76

H

Hairy Persimmon, 57
Hairy Vetch, 145
Halcion, 118
hallucinations, 12
Harrison-Crawford Forestry, 37
Haws, 89
Hay Fever, 105
Heal-all, 110, 146
Heartnuts, 145
Hedeoma pulegioide, 122
Helianthus annuus, 115, 121
Helianthus tuberosus, 91
Hemerocallis fulva, 69
Hemlock trees, 10
Hemorrhoids, 116
Hemp, 139
Henbit, 2, 89
herbicide, 2, 20, 121
Hickory, 53, 89, 127, 140, 165
high blood pressure, 106, 119, 145
Holcus lanatus, 11
honey, 8, 47, 74, 87, 113
Honey Locust, 47, 76
Hoosier Banana, 54
Horse Nettle, 107
horseradish, 25, 47, 85, 92
Horsetail, 106, 110, 141
Huckleberry, 27
Hydrastis canadensis, 122
hydrocyanic acid, 11
Hypericum perforatum, 117, 120

I

Ilex opaco, 86
Illinois, 86, 96, 150, 154
immune enhancer, 120, 146
Impatiens capensis, 107
Impatiens spp., 24
Incas, 23, 72
Indian Cucumber-root, 40
Indian Hemp, 139
Indian Mallow, 2, 127, 139
Indian Strawberry, 2
Indiana, 2, 21, 25, 37, 50, 51, 54, 58, 66, 67, 94, 96, 97, 107, 143, 147, 148, 150, 153, 164
insects, 27, 54, 93, 100, 121, 139
Iris, 15, 31, 80
Iris pseudoacorus, 15, 31
Iris versicolor, 15, 31
Iroquois, 16, 116

J

Jack-in-the-Pulpit, 32, 37, 143
James Whitcomb Riley, 54
Japanese Trapdoor Snails, 145
Jerusalem Artichoke, 65, 91, 145
Jewelweed, 24, 107, 108, 146
Jimson Weed, 109
Johnson Grass, 11
Juglans cinera, 53
Juglans nigra, 53, 110, 121
Juglans spp., 90
Jumbo Bluegill, 145
Juneberries, 145
Juniper, 123, 127

K

Kansas, 57, 86
Kentucky, 47, 76, 86
Kentucky Coffee Tree, 47, 76
Korean Lezbedeza, 145

L

Labiatae, 29
Labiatea, 121
Lactucca spp., 76, 107
Laportea canadensis, 24, 43, 108
Largemouth Bass, 145
Larkspurs, 122
latex, 86, 94
Lauraceae, 86
Laurel, 11, 40, 86
Laurel Greenbrier, 40
Lemon Balm, 79, 118, 146
Leonurus caradiaca, 118
Leopard Frog, 94
lice, 146
Lichens, 141
Lindera benzoin, 37, 86
lobsters, 97, 98
Lolium tamulentum, 11
Lotus, 31, 92
Louisiana, 73, 76, 96, 97
LSD, 12
Lyme Disease, 109
Lyme Spirochetes, 109
lysergic acid diethylamide, 12

M

Maclura pomifera, 122
Ma-huang, 106
Maidenhair Tree, 117
Maple, 2, 74, 90
Marijuana, 139
Matricaria chamomilla, 104
Mayapple, xv, 37, 43, 61, 112, 122, 143
Medeola virginiana, 40
Melissa officinalis, 118

Menispermum canadense, 39, 136
Mentha piperita, 29
Mentha pulegium, 122
Mentha spicata, 29
methyl salicylate, 102
mice, 7
Michigan, 54, 86
Michigan Banana, 54
migraine, 12
Milkweed, 112, 127, 139, 145
minnow, 98
Mint, 29, 122
Mississippi, 10, 54, 120, 135
Missouri, 86
moccasin, 94
mollusk shell, 128, 129
Monarda didyma, 110
mono matate, 12
Morel, 47
Mormon Tea, 106, 117
Mormons, 106
Mosquito, 122
Motherwort, 118
Mountain Mint, 27, 122, 146
Mountain Pepperbush, 135
Mulberry, 2
Mullein, 2, 112, 116, 117, 135, 138, 141, 145
mushrooms, xv, xviii, 53
Mustard, 2, 25, 73, 85

N

Nanking Cherries, 145
Narcissus, 69
Narrow-leaved Plantain, 108
Nasturtiums, 145
Native Americans, 1, 3, 7, 8, 12, 37, 101, 107, 109, 110, 112, 115, 121, 123, 128, 130, 131, 134, 135, 137
nausea, 145
nettle, 133
Nettle Soup, 24
New Jersey Tea, 77, 135
nightshade, 107
NIH, 117
nitrate, 23, 68
Nodding Wild Onion, 62
norpseudoephedrine, 106, 117
Nuphar advena, 31
Nuphar variegatum, 31
Nutrition Enhancers, 20, 22, 72, 118

O

Oak, 7, 8, 53, 76, 107, 127, 140
Oenothera biennis, 73, 85, 139
Ohio, 135, 148, 157
Omaha, 135
Omega-3 fatty acids, 68, 120
Onion, 80, 109
Ontario, 54, 86

opossum, 58, 87
Opuntia, 7, 21, 90, 109, 119, 136, 145
Opuntia humifusa, 21, 136
Opuntia spp., 90, 109, 119
Oriental Ginseng, 120
Osage-Orange, 122
Ostrich, 41
oxalate acid crystals, 32
oxalic acid, 23, 68
Oxalis spp., 80

P

Pale Purple Coneflower, 117
Pan Scrubbers, 141
Panax ginseng, 120
Panax quinquefolius, 111, 120
parsnips, 85
Pawnee, 135
Pawpaw, 54, 55, 56, 110, 123
Pecan, 53
Peltandra virginica, 32
Pennyroyal, 27, 122, 145
pens, 12, 96
Peppergrass, 65, 73
Peppermint, 2, 29
Permaculture, 144, 146, 150
Persian Walnut, 145
Persimmon, 57, 58, 60, 77, 104, 153, 157, 159
Peruvian, 23
pesticide, 2, 144
pharmacopeia, 110
Phragmites, 12, 31, 33, 75
Phragmites communis, 12, 33
Phragmites spp., 75
phytochemical, 119
Phytolacca americana, 65
phytolaccin, 66
Pickerel Frog, 94
Pickerelweed, 32
Pilea pumila, 43
Pine Needle Tea, 90
Pine Needles, 10
Pine nuts, 10, 24
Pine Pitch, 128, 129
Pine Pollen, 10
Pines, 7, 9, 11, 90, 127
Pinyon Pines, 145
Plantago lanceolata, 108, 115
Plantago spp., 104
Plantain, 65, 89, 90, 104, 108, 115, 119, 138
Podophyllum peltatum, 37, 43, 61, 112, 122
Poison Hemlock, xv, 31, 81
Poison Ivy, 39, 50, 74, 107, 138, 146
poison look-alikes, xvii, 5, 47, 69
Poison Oak, 80, 107
Poison Sumac, 74, 80, 107
Poke, 2, 65, 66, 67
Pokeweed, 65
Pollution Indicators, 141

Polygonatum spp., 43
Polyporus sulphurus, 53
Pomo, 7
Ponca, 135
pond, 34, 95, 145
Pontederia cordata, 32
Portulaca oleracea, 2, 68, 73, 108, 120
Portulacaceae, 68
Possum, 99
poultice, 22, 103, 104, 109
Prickly Lettuce, 2
Prickly Pear Cactus, 21, 90, 109, 119
Prunella vulgaris, 103, 110, 120
pseudoephedrine, 106, 117
Psyllium seed, 115
Pteretis aquilinum, 41
Pteretis pensylvanica, 41
Puffballs, 2
Purple Coneflower, 105, 109, 117, 120, 145
Purslane, 2, 65, 68, 71, 73, 108, 120
Pussy Willow, 102
Pycnanthemum muticum, 122
Pyrethrum, 122
Pyrus spp., 86

Q

Queen Anne's Lace, 80
Quercus spp., 7, 53, 84
quills, 12
quinoa, 23

R

Rana catesbeiana, 94
Rana clamitans, 94
Rana palustris, 94
Rana pipiens, 94
Rana sphenocephala, 94
Rape, 25
Raspberries, 26, 53
Red Clover, 2, 77, 113, 145
Red Dock, 72
red oaks, 7
Redbud Tree, 46
Reed, 12, 31, 33, 75, 129
Rennet, 86
Rhus Glabra, 136
Rhus radicans, 107
Rhus spp., 74
Rhus toxicodendron, 107
Rhus vernix, 74, 80, 107
Ringworm, 110
River Birch, 89
Robina pseudo-acacia, 47
Rosemary, 146
Rubus allegheniensis, 29
Rubus occidentalis, 29
Rubus spp., 26, 53, 115
Rumex crispus, 24, 108

Rumex spp., 72
Russian Olive, 2

S

safrole, 37
Sage, 127
Sagittaria spp., 31, 92, 145
Saint John's Wort, 117, 120, 146
salicin, 30, 101
Salix alba, 101, 107
Salix babylonica, 102
Salix nigra, 101
Salix spp., 29, 101
Sambucus canadensis, 67, 74, 122
Sambucus nigra, 117
Sandpaper, 141
Sanguinaria canadensis, 122
sap, 8, 74, 75, 90, 107, 112, 128, 136
Saponaria offinales, 135
sapponins, 23, 71, 135
Sassafras, 37, 73, 77, 84, 86, 127, 138
Sassafras albidum, 37, 73
Saw Palmetto, 21, 139
Scirpus validus, 33
Scott O'Grady, 11
Scout Pit, 133, 134
Sedative, 146
Sedatives, 118
Sedge, 29, 127
Serenoa repens, 21, 139
shrimp, 98
Siberian Ginseng, 120
skin rashes, 146
Slender Arrowhead, 32
Slender Nettle, 24, 43, 108
Smilacina racemosa, 43
Smilax bona-nox, 40
Smilax spp., 40, 75, 84
Smooth Sumac, 90, 136
Snails, 145
snake, 109
snapping turtle, 94, 95, 96
Soap, 135, 146
Soaproot, 135
Solanum carolinense, 107
Sorbus americana, 89
Sorghum, 11, 145
Sorghum halenpense, 11
soup, 16, 24, 33, 84, 96, 129
Spanish Bayonet, 71
Spatterdock, 31
Spearmint, 29
Spicebush, 37, 77, 86, 87, 90, 100, 138, 159, 160
Spider Bites, 109
Spikenard, 51
spiles, 12, 74, 129
spinach, 22, 23
Spirodela polyrhiza, 34
Spring Beauty, 68

Spring Cress, 47, 85
Spring-beauties, 40
Spurge, 71
squirrel, 1
St Anthony's fire, 12
Staghorn Sumac, 74, 80
Star Chickweed, 71
Stellaria media, 2, 71
Stellaria pubera, 71
Stellaria vulgatum, 71
stimulant, 106, 117
Stinging Nettle, 24, 43, 86, 103, 105, 108, 119, 138, 139
stings, 16, 24, 32, 109
styptic, 16, 102, 146
Sulphur Shelf, 53
Sumac, 80, 90, 107, 127
Sunchokes, 91
Sunflower, 91, 115, 121
superfood, 72
Sustainable Agriculture, 144
Sweet Pepperbush, 135
Sweetflag, 15, 31, 84, 119, 122, 128
Sweetgum, 2
Symphytum officinale, 103

T

Tadpoles, 145, 161
tannic acid, 7, 8, 58
Taraxacum offinale, 20, 76, 118
Tea Berry, 102
Teasel, 137
Texas, 54, 57, 97, 156
Texas Persimmon, 57
Thistle, 127
thymol, 110
Tilia americana, 119
Tinea corpis, 110
Tinea cruris, 110
Tinea pedis, 110
Toiletries, 137
Toothworts, 40, 85
torches, 16, 141
touch-me-nots, 107
Transition areas, 29
tree sap, 12, 128
Trichostema lanceolatum, 135
Trichostema spp., 135
Trifolium pratense, 113
Tulip Poplar, 128
Turkey mullein, 135
Turtles, 92, 95
Tussilago farfara, 113
Typha angustifolia, xviii, 15
Typha domingensis, 15
Typha glauca, xviii, 15
Typha latifolia, xviii, 15, 31

U

upset stomach, 109, 114, 145
Utrica dioica, 24, 43, 86, 103, 105, 108, 119, 139
Utrica gracilis, 24, 43, 108

V

Vaccinium corymbosum, 29
Vaccinium macrocarpon, 29
Vaccinium spp., 27, 114
Valerian, 118, 146
Velvet Grass, 11
Velvetleaf, 127, 139
venison, 1, 86
Verbascum thapsus, 112, 116
Vinegar Weed, 135
Vines, 128
Viola odorata, 118
Viola spp., 42, 113, 119
Violet, 113, 118, 146
Virginia, 2, 10, 54, 128, 152, 155, 166
Virginia Creeper, 128
Vitaceae, 39
Vitis spp., 39, 84

W

Walnut, 54, 127, 140
Wapato, 32, 92
Warts, 112
Water Hemlock, 31, 81, 85, 92
Watercress, 31
Watershield, 31
Weeping Willow, 101
White Alder, 135
White Birch, 89
White Pine, 2
White Willow, 101, 107
Wild Allspice, 86
Wild Asparagus, 15, 65, 66, 148, 153
Wild Carrot, xv, 2, 31, 80, 86
Wild Garlic, 79, 114, 117, 119, 121
Wild Ginger, 43, 84, 113, 114, 117, 119
Wild Grapes, 39, 84
Wild Horseradish, 85
Wild Leeks, 47
Wild Lettuce, 107
Wild Oats, 118, 146
Wild Rice, 12, 33
Wild Sarsaparilla, 51
Wild Strawberries, 145
Wild Yam, 143, 145
Willow, 101, 102, 127, 128, 140, 145
Willow basket, 128
Wintercress, 2, 25, 90, 109
Wintergreen, 101, 102
witchcraft, 12
wood ash, 8, 138
Wood Nettles, 24, 43, 50
wood sorrel, 68

wounds, 16, 102, 103

X

Xanax, 118
Xanthium spp., 72

Y

Yarrow, 102, 118, 135, 145, 146
Yellow Bedstraw, 86
Yellow Birch, 89
Yellow Dock, 2, 108
Yellow Flag, 15, 31, 47
Yellow Nut Grass, 29
Yellow Rocket, 25, 90
Yellow Root, 116
Yucca, 71, 110, 123, 127, 134, 135, 139, 146
Yucca aloifolia, 71
Yucca filamentosa, 71, 110, 135
Yucca spp., 71, 135, 139

Z

Zigadenus venenosus, 80
Zingiber offinale, 117
Zizania aquatica, 12, 33

About The Author

Kevin is a retired Naval Officer. He has a BS degree in Biology Education and a Masters Degree in Computer Science. During his career in the Navy, he attended eight wilderness survival courses. While stationed at Fort Meade, Maryland, Kevin served as a volunteer naturalist at the Patuxent Wildlife Refuge where he conducted monthly wild edible plant walks. Upon his retirement from the Navy he returned to his native Indiana where he continued to conduct local wild edible plant walks as well. He has also given talks to Rotary clubs and scout groups. Kevin has published several magazine articles while doing research for his book. Currently Kevin works during the week as a computer consultant and on the weekends he returns home to his 23-acre farm in Greenville, Indiana where he continues to enjoy and learn about nature.

Printed in the United Kingdom
by Lightning Source UK Ltd.
9772300001B/24